MINNE-SOTA ♨ HEAT!

The heat Minnesotans get
when they go someplace else
(talk on the phone even).

And coping from there.

BOB RUEFF

Illustrations by
PETE BASTIANSEN

rm Publishing, Inc.

ISBN 0-9656395-0-9

J   I   H   G   F   E   D   C   B   A

Printed in the United States of America

To Walter,
and all coping Minnesotans.

Acknowledgments

Al Fahden, who critiqued an aimless, redundant draft long before an aimless, redundant book got bound.

Milt Adams, fellow Minneapolis Washburnite, who introduced a neophyte to the publishing world (region, anyway).

Morrie Lundin, University of Minnesota classmate, who formatted *Minnesota Heat* with great forbearance.

Pete Bastiansen, who's cartoons are more Minnesotan than a Minnesota author could have hoped for.

Don Terwilliger, former business partner, and friend, who helped tie the graphic look of these pages together.

Donna Montgomery, who's guidance kept a clueless author on track to distribution.

Lou, who patiently aided and abetted the whole project from the home front.

And, not least, all skulkers out there without whom there'd be no *Minnesota Heat*.

You'd about think we're talking great book, here.

"Minnesotans are different from the rest of us...
Minnesotans recycle...Minnesotans return the
grocery cart to the store. Minnesotans do not
consume butter-fat...Minnesotans bike with
their helmets on. Minnesotans fasten their seat
belts. Minnesotans hold the door open for you.
Minnesota men don't leave the toilet seat up.
Minnesotans do not blow their horns behind
you when the light turns green; they wait for
you to notice."

—*Charles Kuralt's America*

Minnesota Nice: A Minnesota malady. Minnesotans cheer when the visiting team does something good; apologize when their feet get stepped on—deliberately.

Geo-climatic Skulkers: Deliberate steppers.

Contents

Introduction: The Tilted Landscape 1

The Geo-climatic Skulker 7

Heat About Minnesota 13

Winter Cold Heat 21

Summer Heat Heat 31

Springs that aren't. Falls that are. 39

Don't-let-'em-tell-ya's,
    even-though-they-will's 45

First Return Fire: Showing a little
    initiative there 53

Give Backs: Things to Let Up With 71

Minnesota Mindworks
    and other inexplicables 79

Land O'Water 83

Down South 95

"Fargo" 97

Under the Weather. Nothing to Do 99

War of Attrition 109

Minnesota Wraps 121

Minnesota Heat Quick-scan Traveler 125

Keep skulkers at bay at home and away,
    with *Minnesota Heat* Take-alongs 153

Introduction:
The Tilted Landscape.

Minnesotans are different from the rest of the inhabitants of this nation. They're prime patsies, you see. Fair game to other-staters who prey on guileless Minnesota migrants passing their way. Winter, of course, kicking things off.

"You're from Minnesota? HA!", they bluster from below Minnesota borders. "Colder than (select frozen meat locker, well-digger's whatever, witches whatevers, polar far-reaches, sub-zero anythings, brass monkey somethings); mosquitoes bigger than (large predatory bird of choice); summers shorter than (days numbered in single digits); bumpkins duller than (Swedes and/or Norwegians with IQ's numbered in double-digits)."

Minnesotans are accustomed to these fusillades, and in a strange masochistic way, even accepting of it. It's almost as though these admonishments were cleansing an unexpurgated guilt stemming from a choice of habitat—as might be expected living in a state represented by a rodent that dives underground at first provocation, and a bird that takes flight under water. Then there's that slogan, "We like it here," pointing out how self-effacing we can be; plus a state university football team that has long played out how accommodating we can be with our visitors, as well as to those we visit.

Finally, and perhaps most importantly, there's Minnesota Nice contributing to this quandary—a cultural affliction making it nigh impossible for Minnesotans to defend themselves, even when equipped with enough debunking information to do so. Minnesota Nice decrees you grin and bear it—take your licking lest you offend your offender, don't you know.

Now, compare all this with how other-staters mostly come at things and you begin to see the enormity of the condition *Minnesota Heat* has chosen to deal with. Can the gap be narrowed? Can the beleaguered Minnesotan ever hope to salve his beleaguerment—once made *aware* of his beleaguerment in the first place? *Fight back,* even?

Admittedly, *Minnesota Heat's* counsel may unsettle Minnesota psyches quashed by years of on-the-road ritualized floggings. It won't be easy. And it may not be pretty. There's debunking to be done, information to be imparted, ploys to be mastered, new thought to be taught. It's not without psychological hazard that we proceed. But Minnesotans, with the acquiescence we know you have in you, *Minnesota Heat* can set you free. Should you want that, of course.

What *Minnesota Heat* will do for you.

Heighten awareness. You'll see how Geo-climatic Skulkers, identified for you in this treatise, work their wiles—prod you with shivering reminders of winter cold to stifling remembrances of summer humidity—then humble you with back-woods "up-there" routines whittled to piercing perfection. And when not directly besmirching your geographic surroundings, you'll learn how they whipsaw you with contrasting wonderments of their own marvelous environs to finish the carve.

Debunk bunk. Many "truths" are false when it comes to Minnesota *downs*, and other-state *ups*. *Minnesota Heat* debunks the bunk, instilling true truths in their place.

Tutors your tours. Minnesotans are so much putty in the hands of Geo-climatic Skulkers because they know so little about the attributes and contributions of their own state. How many Minnesotans know, for instance, where water skiing started? We'll tell you that, and much, much more.
(Hint: It wasn't Iowa.)

Help you fight back. We know fighting back is oxy-moronic for Minnesotans, but *Minnesota Heat* will show you how to stop Geo-climatic Skulkers in their tracks while still preserving all the submissive imperatives you hold dear.

As a bonus there's a handy *Quick-Scan Traveler* at the back of this book you can refer to at first skulker provocation. You'll be cool with useful facts, figures and debunking data for quick retaliation—Minnesota style. *Minnesota Heat Take-Alongs* are available to you, as well, for augmenting your sojourns elsewhere.

After reading this book you'll *not* have to hang your head in capitulation as they heap it on you one more time (unless you choose to out of practice). You *will* be able to respond with more than: "uh-huh," after each blustering boast tossed your way (though you may choose not to). And, finally, you *can* abandon your besmirched niche in American society (if not too unsettling for you).

MINNESOTANS ARE *NOT REALLY* GULLIBLE —
THEY ARE, HOWEVER, FAIR. YES, THAT'S IT — FAIR.

The Geo-climatic Skulker.

OK we've established you're going to get hit whenever you venture anywhere beyond the 42nd parallel (south to Minnesotans, north to most other folk). Sooner or later, even the most benevolent of out-of-staters is going to take a poke or two. It's just the way it is. But beware the true Geo-climatic Skulker laying in wait for Minnesotans: *Geo* as in geography (yours), *climatic* as in climate (also yours) *Skulker* as in ambusher (him, of you). This is the guy to watch out for—the one who will put it to you mercilessly while enjoying every flay of your hide.

Scanning weather forecasts, checking off days on calendars, scrutinizing The Farmer's Almanac, sniffing the air, Geo-climatic Skulkers lurk at the ready. Golf courses, restaurants, tennis courts, pool-side reposes, collection points ev-

erywhere—they're poised. The second Mississippi Flyway season is about to open. On you!

"Mosquitoes larger than birds," they sting.
You flinch, timorously.

"Humidity you can drown in," they sputter.
You choke, concedingly.

"Nine months of hibernation," they growl.
You hunker, bearingly.

"Backwoods," they howl.
You cower, whimpingly.

"Windchills to Absolute Zero," they blow.
You hunch, chillingly.

"Ten months of snow—two months of poor
sledd'n," they push.
You skid to final defeat.

Lets face it, Minnesotans are hubris-feeding
fodder for Geo-climatic Skulkers. In many climes
the great Minnesota bash has been polished to
an art form, California, Arizona, Texas, and
Florida skulkers being its virtuosos. But even
northern-tier brethren have skulkers who join
the chorus:

Chicagoan (amid swirling winds, and a four-
degree average temperature disparity with
Minneapolis) cackles: "So cold they close it
down."

Detroiter (amid shin-deep slush) coughs:
"You sure get a lot of white stuff up there."

New Yorker (amid life-threatening chaos) chokes: "So dull they close it down." (Well, at least it's not related to weather.)

Yes, Minnesota patsyism runs deep and Geo-climatic Skulkerism thrives on it. Skulkers everywhere instinctively sense Minnesota Nice— that Minnesota affliction instilled in childhood: "Be polite." "Smile sweet." "Share your candy." "Say thank you." "When someone sasses you— roll over."

The apology-at-the-ready Minnesotans carry with them is glaring on skulker turf where nothing approaching it has ever gone before. Geo-climatic Skulkers can scent and track a white-eyed Minnesotan from 50 paces, easy. Not that they have to. Minnesotans wander right into their sights. Every winter.

Awash in jingoistic fervor, skulkers do not share the characteristics they so readily exploit. Nor does it remotely matter at all to them that their boasts and brickbats may lack foundation as often as not:

> Arizona does *not* have the most golf courses per capita, as Arizonans assume.

> California did *not* give birth to Roller Blades, as Californians are prone to think.

> Florida is *not* the home of water skiing, as Floridians pre-suppose.

Texas does *not* have more boats than any-where else, as Texans boastingly claim.

California, Texas and Florida put together do *not* have the most shoreline of the lower 48 states, as each state will individually exhort.

Guess who's ahead of them, in each instance? Can it be...? Nawww. Bulldozed, the Minnesotan cows: "Golly gee, this place (wherever he is out-side of Minnesota) sure is somethin', aw right."

Its not fair: *They're* raised in vainglory. *You're* raised in excuse-me's. If *Minnesota Heat* can change all that, just consider the long-term benefits that can be yours. Soon you'll drop from the sights of other-staters not wanting to put up with retorts, much less the glimmerings of messy truths you now possess—*supportable* truths at that. No Siree. Not while easier booty's to be had.

Skulkers out there will move to easier prey, you'll see. Dropped like a Minnesota hotdish, you'll sink into divine oblivion—able to pass through habitats where once you were game on the hoof. Anonymous. Ignored. Forgotten. Phased to blankness. A Minnesota dream come true.

Unsuspecting Iowans will now don concentric circles on their backs out of default, ignorantly (as Iowans are prone) assuming your former place in the preyful scheme of things. The tormentor's won't be denied, they'll simply turn to where game is more plentiful. They can't help themselves. It's *their* heritage.

OK, there'll be those of you who feel it's your *right* to be goaded. Play the apologist. Suffer the taunts of 48 states (Iowa, not counted). Tenaciously cling to whip-ee status. You earned it, you assert—the only thing you *ever* asserted. If that's your wont, *Minnesota Heat* can't do anything for you. But if, on the other hand, you're one of the more courageous Minnesota souls, minority though you may be, there's help to be had.

"MOSQUITOES BIG ENOUGH TO SHOOT"

"HUMIDITY YOU CAN DROWN IN"

"NINE MONTHS OF HIBERNATION"

"WIND CHILLS TO ABSOLUTE 'O'"

Heat About Minnesota.

A ny discussion having to do with Minnesota invariably starts with cold weather. It will ever be so when uttering those fateful words beyond these borders: *"I'm from Minnesota."*

The typical response to that admission is "Brrrrr," usually delivered with mock shuddering of grave discomfort. As calculated, this immediately puts the hapless Minnesotan on the defensive—clearly illustrating that where he resides is far less desirable than where the other person resides. This single measure, cold weather, is supreme. It's the Litmus Test. Nothing else matters a whit. Not crime, not corruption, not cultural neglect, not crumbling infrastructure, not moral decay, not societal failings, not political shenanigans. Nor does any other indigenous ill besetting the other-stater's habitat mean beans,

no matter how grievous or of what magnitude. Certainly not to the Geo-climatic Skulker. The hapless Minnesotan, knowing he's faced with these ruling guidelines of discussion, has no viable retort. The Minnesotan is skewered before he can utter, "Nice day, here."

Snowbirds? Well, of course you are, Minnesotans. This less than laudatory term is reserved expressly for you, and accepted by you, as you go about preserving the local economy of your captious hosts. But, what about those same folk venturing north to escape the insufferable heat never acknowledged, come summer? Desert Rats, perhaps? Gulf Geese? How 'bout Prune Faces? Sun Spots? Glade Runners? Maybe Dust Mites? May we suggest any one of these labels is as appropriate as Snowbird is for Minnesota trekkies during winter months. But Nooo... Minnesota Nice or, to-be-taken-advantage-of naiveté, doesn't allow for that. These refugees from scorchtown are *vacationers,* whose visiting duty it is to remind Minnesotans of humidity, mosquitoes and snow-dumps soon to arrive, lest you fall into some kind of summer-time complacency. Then, after commenting numberless times of weird Minnesota accents, those visitors will depart at first sight of a falling leaf with: "Y'all come down freezn' time, hee'ya?", while tremulously clutching their shoulders in a cross-armed body hug for "freezn' time" emphasis.

Minnesota home field advantage in summer? Forget it. Level playing field in winter? Not a chance. Not when one side is culturally challenged to begin with and, at least half the time, doesn't know it's even in the game.

Minnesotans come honestly by their happenstance. They've earned it, and *learned* it. For months on end, Minnesotans dutifully absorb ominous winter-weather messages of impending gravity only mad wolves and Scandinavians could hope to endure.

It's not that Minnesotans are spared by their local weather casters during summer either (which we'll get to in a later chapter) but with the first inklings of winter things really get shrill. From baleful bed-time newscasts following on the heels of the first frost warning, one hardly dares reach out for the morning paper on the front stoop. And should the newspaper be successfully retrieved before threatened hypothermia sets in, it will serve to perpetuate dire warnings of sub-zero horrors yet to befall the timorous reader—this time, over breakfast. Advertisers do it to us, too. A local ad brought urgency to its October Sale saying: "Hurry. This offer won't last as long as the eight months of winter ahead." The *Star Tribune*, Minnesota's big newspaper, requested its readers to send in "scary winter stories" they've had. "Has there been a time when the winter weather has really scared you?", it asked. And, if scary enough, they promised to print it. And they did. Gee, we can hardly wait to read about how terrifying things can be for us up here.

Official temperatures are normally reported from a spot in a community chosen for representative accuracy—shielded from the sun, positioned several feet above ground level. So how is it done in the Twin Cities? Well, it seems there's this "hole" out there at Minneapolis/St. Paul International Airport from which measurements are extracted, off one of the runways where planes won't run into it. You may wonder, why a "hole," a magnet for cold air said to produce all sorts of temperature extremes which (surprise) do not appear on *unofficial* monitors placed elsewhere around here, was selected? Or, for that matter, why is the blamed thing located at the airport, away from the city, in the first place? Well, you see, large cities generate a lot of heat in themselves and, just because that's where people actually live, they wouldn't want to report temperatures from there, now would they. The deep plunging gyrations that result from all this are a lot more fun to report. It's a Minnesota thing.

Yes, Minnesotans are weather-beaten long before fleeing south on I-35 or evacuating themselves on a Northwest gray-bellied red-tail—the only bird still flying not having migrated for the duration.

Nothing seems to help. Take the summer and fall of 1996, for example. From June through August, Minneapolis-St. Paul highs averaged a pleasant 80 degrees. Humidity levels and Dewpoints were commodious to a fault. Rains sprinkled accommodatingly at night or in the wee hours of the morning. The sun shown brightly most waking hours, bringing ancillary warmth which gentle breezes then soothed. September's song was a repeating refrain. October greeted most Minnesotans with 75 and sunny. Twin Cities Marathoners finished their urban parkway trek the following weekend in flawless environs. Two hundred and fifty miles to the north, fall colors exploding, Minnesotans plied Superior National under ideal golfing conditions. Highs in the mid 70's ranged across the state the weekend after that. In a fit of objective commentary, the *Star Tribune* wrote :

> *"The passages at dawn and dusk are filled with that particular golden glow of mid-October that makes each leaf seem lighted from within...Is the sunlight softer in the mornings or the evenings? By the creek or by the lake? Which glows with more apparent candlepower: a scarlet maple leaf or a yellow one? How many more perfect days will 1996 provide?"*

All this left Minnesota weather casters bereft—no atmospheric episodes to frighten us with all this time. It was five-plus months of weatherly bliss— likely the friendliest climactic happenings on the Planet. What were Minnesotans to do? Nary a cosmic episode to fret about, feel deprived of, apologize for? You offered "Nice summer," to your tundra brethren and likely got a questioning "Yeah," as though there must still be some over-sight not coming to mind at the moment. But what? *Well, it was kinda hot that one Saturday. It rained after the car got washed. The grass grew kinda fast. A pesky gnat had to be shooed...*

So, you see, it's not just weather casters to blame. It's the norm for Minnesotans to focus on their indigenous negatives with bewildering relish, dwelling on them at every opportunity:

- Windchill, hail, sleet, humidity—weather in general.
- Mosquitoes, gnats, ticks, June Beetles—bugs in general.
- Crabgrass, dandelions, milfoil, golden rod—weeds in general.
- Road work, potholes, bottle necks, entry and exit-ramp line-ups—roads in general.
- Rust, fungus, mildew, timber-rot—entropy in general.
- Bland, tasteless, textureless, lutefisk—food in general.
- Vy-queens, Twinkies, Woofies, No Stars, Golden Rodents—local sports in general.
- Politics. Well—Minnesota politics in general.

C'mon now, tell the truth. Have you not shared with your neighbors such wayward, hinterland topics? Now compare this with how other-state skulkers come at things and you begin to see the enormity of the schism between you and *them.*

Nobody said this would be easy.

Winter Cold
Heat.

It's not to say temperatures never reach below the most friendly during the hippodrome of winter in Minnesota. But are things really so dire as reputed? *Minnesota Heat* says not, and offers some perspectives to keep in mind when next you're being inundated with winter bombast's, home or away—which will occur just as surely as the brown bear seeks refuge in the Minnesota woods.

This time, before you run off to your annual pummeling grounds below these borders, there are some things you should be made aware of— even though you think you know all there is to know about Minnesota winters. A case in point: Wanna take a stab at what the mean mid-day thermometer reads in Minneapolis-St. Paul, January through February, the two coldest months of the year? We're talking the times of day when folks are out and about doing their thing, not three o'clock in the morning when they're snuggled up all cozy in bed. Ah-ah, no peeking ahead, now. C'mon, you're a Minnesotan, you know about such things, don't you?. Close your eyes and give it your best shot. Write it down. OK, Ready? According to the National Weather Service (if you can't trust your government agencies, what can you trust?) the mean high temperature for these two nasty months is, 23.6 degrees F. That's *above* zero, Frosty. For December it's 26.6 degrees F. For March it's 37 degrees F. Surprised? How much did you miss January-February by? And would you have guessed it for December? Or March? *Minnesota Heat* is betting your forecasts in each case were on the less-hospitable side. If *you're* wrong—a true blue Minnesotan—just how far off do you expect your run-of-the-mill skulker to be? Try 'em next time out, why don't you—now that you know the answer isn't as frightful as the perception.

The Windchill Factor.

Most Minnesotans live in abject fear of Windchills. Heaven knows, they've been given cause, what with warnings as abundant as icy projectiles in a sleet storm. Now, we realize most Minnesotans are reluctant to question their anointed weather authorities who beat on them with Windchill reports until they really do turn blue. But, incredulous as it may seem, Windchills—the heart and soul of winter's scare—do not live up (or down) to their promised calamity. Consider *these* factors:

1. Windchill isn't really a temperature at all. Besides scaring the bejezzes out of you every day and handing skulkers a fused missile to hurl at you, it's a made-up formula based on how fast heat is carried away from your body should you stand in the middle of an open prairie bare-butt naked. Not a likely event.

2. Winds gust and ebb. Windchill, therefore, is not the unremitting terror so deliciously built into your multi-day weather forecasts, even if you are standing in that field with no clothes on. Sometimes it's not there at all.

3. Now, what if you should be shielded from the wind by a building, tree or other such fortuitous obstruction? Or wearing clothing, for heavens sake. Or what if you're moving (skiing, jogging, hiking, walking) in the same direction as those grisly gusties? Does Windchill hold its promised devastation then? Of course not.

4. Then there's the never-mentioned radiant heat of the sun, which *Minnesota Heat* calls the Sun Sear Factor (if not us, who?) which is the exact opposite of Windchill, and works to counter its effects. You see, when the sun is shining directly on you it *creates* heat, compensating, at least in part, for the dreaded Windchill's take-away effect on your tender pelt. The Sun Sear Factor may be less in January than it is in March when the sun is higher in the sky, but it's still there, working

SKULKER WELCOMING MINNESOTA
"SNOWBIRD" UPON HIS FLIGHT FROM
THE DREADED WINDCHILL.

for your snuggy betterment. Where are re-ports to this end? Gracious, you might even feel better about your pitiful plight. We can't have *that*. And what about skulkers? They'd be seriously deprived, not hearing the worst about your miserable situation up here, or putting it to you down there.

All considered, winters in Minnesota are nicely usable, don't you think? They offer a world of recreation. It's not just brown-out time as it is in a lot of other places around the country. Have you been to New York in the winter? Washington DC? New Orleans? Have you experienced winter rain across the south? Gone to London or to Paris at that time of the year?

You might even offer an occasional "It's not so bad because...." Or a, "Did you know that...." rebuttal to skulkers, from what you've gleaned here so far. See, we *are* making progress.

Snowed.

Outsiders have a hard time understanding the special relationship Minnesotans have with snow, requisite complaining aside. Especially a sizable dump—you know, the kind that calls for 92-point headlines around the nation. Folks elsewhere assume snowfalls make Minnesotans feel bad, and that makes *them* feel good. "I'm glad I don't live there," they get to say in places where earthquakes, mud slides, giant sink holes, brush and/or forest fires, smog, and

HARVEY P. OF KENWOOD,
MPLS. BELONGS TO THIS
SNOW FLAKE CLUB OF MINN.
THEIR GOAL IS TO BE THE FIRST
MAN (WOMEN ARE ALLOWED
IN — BUT NONE HAVE ASKED.) TO
CATCH THE FIRST SNOWFLAKE OF
THE SEASON.

hurricanes are part of life at home. Given these potentials for disaster, Minnesotans are supposed to be scared of *snowflakes?*

Be that as it may, feeling good about Minnesotans assumed to be feeling bad about snow is a regular thing with sunbelters. That's because they naturally assume any drop of white stuff reported anywhere in the United States is taking place in Minnesota. When Boston, New York, Washington DC, along with much of the east, got shut down by the "Blizzard of '96," Minnesotans got the usual calls sympathizing with their snowy predicament. Minnesotans, who had seen nary a flake from the storm, are accustomed to this—along with the disbelief they get on the other end of the line while vainly attempting to explain the offending front is 1,300 miles away.

Of course, Minnesota does get a generous drop every once and again—like happened in the Twin Cities in 1991, and western Minnesota in 1997. In Minnesota, after a dump like that you can pretty much bank on clear skies and bright sun the next day. And something else. The thing that so often happens after one of these aerial events: adults frolicking around out there like kids at a carnival, commiserating with each other and generally extolling their fellow beings as they shovel themselves out.

When we witnessed hard-bitten New Yorkers giving each other high-five's on network television on a relatively dreary "next day" in '96—you

MINNESOTANS HAVE LEARNED TO
CELEBRATE SNOW.

can imagine what it's like in a Minnesota setting. A bounteous snowfall? Its not the worst. It can be the best—the glory of winter.

So next time you get dumped on about winters in Minnesota, smile at the unknowing soul. Then relate a few things culled from *Minnesota Heat.* He won't be interested, and his eyes will quickly glaze over, but the subject will change. Though you'll stand to be labeled a know-it-all after tossing out a few morsels of truth, it's the price you may have to pay for personal redemption.

Now we know this is all coming at you pretty fast. And, as a bona fide Minnesotan, you may even miss being hammered on to some degree. So just parcel things out at first, until such time as you feel secure and comfortable with your elevating lot in life.

Who knows, you may even convince yourself not to flee one of these winters. OK—we haven't offered arguments *that* convincing.

Summer Heat
Heat.

O nly in Minnesota can the coldest spot on earth become the most miserably hot spot on earth—an absolute truth to your other-state intimidators. The reason offered for this mammoth swing is that old standby, humidity. *It's not the heat, its the humidity,* the saying goes. And goes. And goes. What Windchill is to Minnesota-long winters, humidity is to Minnesota-short summers. After all, it's indisputable meteorological science, isn't it? How many times have forecasters pumped it into your sodden brain? You really can't blame bombastic Arizonans or hectoring Californians for laying it on you—you believe it yourself.

Wringing out humidity.

Phoenicians whose *dry* heat doesn't prevent them from abandoning paradise any which way they can between the bookend months of May and October, take major delight in using humidity to show there's absolutely no justification for residing in Minnesota—winter *or* summer. Not while there's a Valley of the Sun beckoning. Then you're flogged with that 9% humidity bit—like ultra-low humidity is something wonderful Minnesotans are fated to do without. Yes, Minnesotans get a lot of heat from humidity.

But, think about that 9% jubilance for a moment. Where do you set your humidifier in winter, when humidity plunges to those low levels in your home? From 30 to 40 percent, that's where. Why? Because that's where humidity *should* be. At a *minimum.* So your lips don't chafe, your throat doesn't catch, your membranes don't crinkle, your eyes don't scratch, your fingers don't crack, your nose doesn't bleed, and your furniture doesn't collapse.

At the other extreme we have an east/west line from Florida to Texas. Folks there worry little about one's body crumbling to dust during summer. You, as a visitor from up North somewhere, will at least not have to contend with the dry heat ruse. Not from this populace. Along this soggy underbelly air is so saturated you can wet a sponge just by waving it over your head. Sheets of paper not pinned down at their edges curl into spit balls. A squeegeed window will fill half a bucket. You can skid down sidewalks like a kid on a Minnesota ice patch. Here you can say it's the heat *and* the humidity.

So where does Minnesota fit between these two humidity extremes of desert and soggy under-belly? Well, comfortably between, we'd say.

Dew Point Doom.

Minnesota meteorologists, deprived of stinging Windchills all summer long, have come up with a devilish instrument of mental torture to bridge that gap—the Dew Point. A witch's brew of heat and humidity stirred to a boil, the Dew Point is a marvelous device for weather forecasters to wield. If the Dew Point registers in the 60's, that's not good, say they. If it bumps into the 70's, take warning, they warn. Should the Dew Point find its way into the 80's you're to seek immediate cover, they cry. And if, God forbid, Dew Points rise above 90, it's too much for hu-man lenity—a word you don't want to know the meaning of. Unfortunately for us, the Dew Point *always* lodges in one of those four brackets from June 15 to September 15 in Minnesota. (Well, almost.) If it didn't (almost) we wouldn't have it, now would we? The saving grace: Minnesotans, as well as other-staters, don't know what the heck a Dew Point is—though it's only a matter of time, we're afraid.

Lest Dew Point highs lay you low, let *Minnesota Heat* offer up some salvaging perspectives.

- First: Let's just say that Dew Points are a little overstated as a measure of impending doom, kinda like Windchills at the other end of the seasonal spectrum. How 'bout re-calibrating five degrees up those horror-scale brackets for starters, weather people? C'mon, give us a break. We'll all feel better. You, too, even.

• Second: What happened to wind in this equation—you know, those breezes that cool and refresh? Those very zephyrs wildly touted as heat-robbing body-savaging, danger-filled lechers of life and breath when flung at us as Windchills all winter long. Why aren't they called up as a "cooling factor" in summer—adding comfort they so cruelly extracted the other half of the year? But need we ask? This is still Minnesota, don't forget—where weather forecasters reign, and you are rained upon. "Keep the air moving," says NSP, one of the nations bigger electric utilities, in an ad telling of low-cost ways to save energy and remain cool in your home during summer. "With only a 2-mph wind, you will feel as cool at 82 degrees as you feel in calm air of 78 degrees," it affirms. Create a "windchill effect" in order to reduce the need for air conditioning, it advises. If not your weather person, your utility will tell you.

Sun Sear Searings.

A mid-summer day of a mere 115 is no more than balmy, say desert denizens, because it's dry. And a summer day of 80 where *you* hail from is stifling because it's not, they add. But wait up, cactus breath: since official temperature is taken *out* of the sun (and four feet from the ground), isn't there something missing here besides humidity relating to bottom-line human comfort? Oh, yeah—there's the Sun Sear Factor, yet to be reckoned with. Put on your shades pardner, we're gonna take a look at what that little ol' factor means to creatures other than gila monsters, sidewinders and scorpions.

Unlike the comforting warmth the Sun Sear Factor brings to Minnesota, it can really sizzle your bacon in Macon, or anywhere else south of the Mason Dixon Line. Exactly how much more does that reported 115 degrees become with the Arizona sun boring down on your shriveling body from directly overhead? You know, that same sun that's waving asphalt streets and rotting tires off vehicles. The same sun that's grounding aircraft with air cooked too thin for lift-off. The same sun forcing Valley denizens to plan out-door activities in wee hours prior to sunrise, or long after sunset. Place a thermometer out in that sun and see how it registers, why don't you? Fry eggs on the sidewalk? It only takes 125 degrees Fahrenheit to do that. Your eggs will be ready right quick, Pard. Sunny side up.

Yes, Sun Sear can be chilling. And being so, you might think Arizonans would be pelted daily with its dangers via *their* local meteorologists, like Minnesotans are flailed with Windchills by theirs. No way, hombre. They're not telling *themselves* much less the rest of the world. It's an unwritten law. The code o' the cactus. Ask an Arizonan: How was summer? Then ask a Minnesotan: How was winter? One is from "paradise" you understand. The other is from, well...somewhere north of there. Guess the spins you'll get.

You may wonder why Sun Sear is not as discomforting during a Minnesota summer as it is in points south. The answer, oh fair-skinned one, lies in the sun's angle in the sky—it's not nearly so direct up on the tundra as it is on the vista. Ol' Sol has to slice through a whole lot of screening atmosphere before reaching your bod up north, from his summertime roost overhead. It's simple geometry. You may not get as powerful a tan way up here, but latitude is keeping the Minnesota sun this side of scathing. Also—there are occasional *clouds* in Minnesota.

So next time you're told how *their* summer heat is more tolerable than *your* summer heat, ask that person to give you a mid-summer weather report by cellular phone while standing in the mid-day sun down there. That won't be static you'll hear, it'll be the sound of lips cracking.

Should you need more persuasion, you can put the Sun Sear Factor to the test yourself. When visiting the sunbelt city of your choice between June and September, do the following:
Just sit a spell in the shade of an olive tree. You'll probably find it tolerable (depending on ambient temperature, Dew Point and, let's call it, Breeze-away, that day).

Then, after 20 minutes or so, move out into the direct sun for an equal amount of time before retreating (walk, don't run) back into the shade.

The official air temperature, as we've said, is the same whether you're in the sun or out of it. But while your shaded perch was tolerable you'll quickly find your unshaded spot is not. What happened? The Sun Sear happened. And now you know.

As a precaution, you may want to do this wearing white, not dark, clothing. Sun Sear and things dark are not a healthy blend. Your chances of surviving a moment or two longer (enabling rescue should it come to that) will be greater wearing white. And you'll escape having to undergo the dreaded dark-shirt detachment procedure—a process best avoided by those with a humble threshold of pain.

> **Warning:** Do not attempt without hydrogenated physician (in shade). Do not attempt at home (Minnesota)—nothing will happen.

So see Minnesotans, you haven't got it so bad, after all. Do we detect a small lift of the head, there? It's *Minnesota Heat*, isn't it? We told you so. This is potent material. Best put it aside for awhile. Rest up a bit. And think about how far you want to go with this whole thing.

Springs that aren't.
Falls that are.

There are two things to be kept in mind with our less-known and, therefore, less-notorious Minnesota seasons: spring and fall. First, there really *is* no spring in Minnesota. It's only deemed to exist in order to comply with those squiggly markings on nationally distributed calendars, and to otherwise signify it's time for Minnesotans to throw open their windows and venture outside without a jacket come heck or high water, the latter being likely. Second, fall doesn't get any better. *Anywhere.*

Minnesota Heat understands you will accept what we've said about spring with an agreeing nod, but may blanch at our unabashed characterization of fall, accuracy aside. So in deference to your Minnesota sensitivities, we'll offer instead: fall is a pretty darn good season, all things considered, that comes just prior to winter's cold. There—all right, now?

Spring. On Occasion.

Actually, spring *does* make an appearance in Minnesota—once every 9 or 11 years. Like clockwork. In between those years, a sort of non-season shows up for a day or two before you're slung directly from winter into summer. One day you're on a toboggan run, the next you're catching rays on the beach. Sometimes that happens with a little stutter step in there. In the decade in which spring really does appear, either your tobogganing or ray-catching will be cut short for the year—Minnesotans never know which it will be.

Normally, what passes for spring in Minnesota is much like the gray period that passes as winter throughout most of the nation. How can a Minnesotan best handle this phenomenon when conversing with other-staters? *Minnesota Heat* suggests you simply don't bring spring up at all. Non-Minnesotans assume you have it like other Americans (albeit later and cooler). And, for the most part, spring is not something you'll have to contend with in discourse. Like a sleeping dog, let it lie.

This brings up an interesting point, though. What in the world do other folk do during the grays of winter they go through in much of the country? Downhill Ski? No. Cross-country Ski? No. Snowboard. No. Snowmobile? No. Skate? No. Snow Shoe though woods? No. Sleigh ride? No. Recreate outdoors at all? Well...no. Hmmm. To be fair, it isn't always just barren ground under foot in those climes. Sometimes there's slush to plod around in.

Fall Forever.

What more can be said about fall in Minnesota. But for the usual predictions of an approaching "mother of all winters" (Californians, this is always to be *our* Big One), fall in Minnesota is, let's face it...perfect. No heat, no cold, no humidity, no rain, no mosquitoes, no ants—not even visiting skulkers (who have all returned home by now), to niggle you.

Unlike spring, fall shows up as scheduled. From Labor Day to Halloween, and sometimes beyond.

It starts with Minnesota's "get-together", a great state fair by any measure. The world's "most beautiful urban marathon" runs its course, of course. Oktober Fests, harvest celebrations of all sorts, and old-fashioned family outings hold forth amid ripe fields of pumpkins and stalks of gold. And all the while an incredible color palette sweeps its magic from the Boundary Waters and Superior National Forest, spreading down across countless lake shores, rolling landscapes, fruited valleys and majestic overseeing bluffs to the south.

Crisp, clear air. Autumnal fragrances. Sunlight castings uniquely "fall". Glowing warmth on your shoulders. Lazy zephyrs wisping your hair. Sky-blue lakes and lake-blue skies tantalizing your senses. It's then you know—*this is God's country.*

There. *Minnesota Heat* has said it for you. Catch your breath, Minnesotans.

But with all our waxing, fall in Minnesota, like spring, is a season best left alone in discourse with aliens. Who's going to believe you? At best, you'll only be accused of plucking from the jingo-book *they* use so often and well. Besides, fall here follows much too positive a script for Minnesotans to handle well in any discussion with outsiders.

For the reasons given, *Minnesota Heat* will skip over spring and fall (for worse and for better) while being mindful of summer and winter (they're the only seasons you're going hear about, anyway) while proceeding with the many other Minnesota matters needing deliverance from skulker pejoratives. Just so you know.

WHAT'S SO GREAT ABOUT MINNESOTA!

RUNNING IN THE WOODS IN AUTUMN.

Don't-let-'em-tell-ya's, even-though-they-will's.

B efore moving on, there are some weather related *don't-let-'em-tell-ya's, even-though-they-will's*, you'll want to be prepared for next time out. You've heard it all before, you just didn't know how to respond to it before:

"The last time I was in Minneapolis, it was 50 below."

The record cold for Minneapolis is minus 34 degrees. It happened a while ago. Still pretty cool, but hardly -50. (Funny, but on that mythical day every one in America was passing through town).

"Minneapolis (St. Paul) is the coldest spot on the face of America."

OK, International Falls, whose temperatures are trumpeted throughout the land by a gleeful media, does get down there a bit. It should be noted, though, that the Minneapolis-St. Paul metropolitan area, domicile to more than half of Minnesota's residents, is some 300-plus miles to the south. Minneapolis-St. Paul isn't listed among Coldest Cities by the National Center for Educational Statistics—nor Snowiest, nor Windiest, nor Wettest. So there!

"All you can do all winter long is hibernate up there."

Hold on, moosehead. With more indoor tennis courts than any other state, Minnesotans never stop running around their backhands. The thousands of miles of cross-country ski trails and snowmobile trails lacing the state (also more than anywhere else) are not neglected, either. Then there's ice fishing on those 10,000 plus lakes, snow shoeing, winter hiking, sledding, downhill skiing, snow-boarding, and indoor and outdoor ice skating on more rinks than you can shake a Christian Brothers hockey stick at. And hundreds of thousands take part in the celebrated St. Paul Winter Carnival activities each year, with its ice sculptures and ice palaces that would make Walt Disney proud. In 1992, the particularly spectacular 166 ft. Winter Carnival Ice Palace drew 2.5 million visitors without any thought of hibernation.

"Earthquakes, smirthquakes—we don't have tornadoes to dodge," Californians are especially quick to assert.

Are we talking Minnesota here? Or are we talking Texas, Oklahoma, Kansas, Missouri, Nebraska, or Iowa—you know, Tornado Alley—a bit to the south. There are 1,000 tornadoes in the U.S. each year, give or take a couple of hundred. Every state has them. Californians *do* have to dodge a few—perhaps a small inconvenience, what with mud slides, brush fires, coastal collapses *plus* earthquakes to dance around. Minnesota's average annual tornado count is a small portion of the nation's total. Sixteen is the normal number that may require some dodging when there's someone around to do it—not always a given when you consider more than half the state lies in pastures and open crop land, a third in forests, and nearly a tenth is open water.

IN MINNESOTA, WE DON'T
HAVE EARTHQUAKES.
DARN!

Of course, you *can* dodge tornadoes, if not rec-
ommended sport. On the other hand, how do
you dodge an earthquake?

*"So Minnesota has a few golf courses. You can
only play three months out of the year."*

Bad swing. Minnesotans in metropolitan Minneapolis-St. Paul can expect to ply the sticks from
mid-April to mid-October. No problem. That
amounts to six months, with some extend-time
at either end. And, Minnesota does have more
than a few courses—like the most per capita of
any state in the union next to North Dakota,
which only has a handful of capita. Minnesota
has more than a few golfers to play 'em, too.
More than 20% of Minnesota residents participate in golf—one of only two states to exceed
that level. By comparison: 13.5% of Arizonans,
10.9% of Californians, 10% of Floridians, and
9.1% of Texans are golfing participants. Fore!

*"Only lumberjacks and hockeypucks thrive in
Minnesota."*

Minnesota's got what skulkers call *culcha*. There
are more theater companies per capita in Minneapolis-St. Paul than any other American city.
And there are more theater goers per capita in
the Twin Cities than in any metro area other
than New York. The Guthrie Theater, in Minneapolis, is regarded as the top regional repertory
theater in the nation. The St. Paul Chamber
Orchestra is the only full-time chamber orchestra in the land. There's The Minnesota Opera
Company, The Minnesota Orchestra, Rochester's

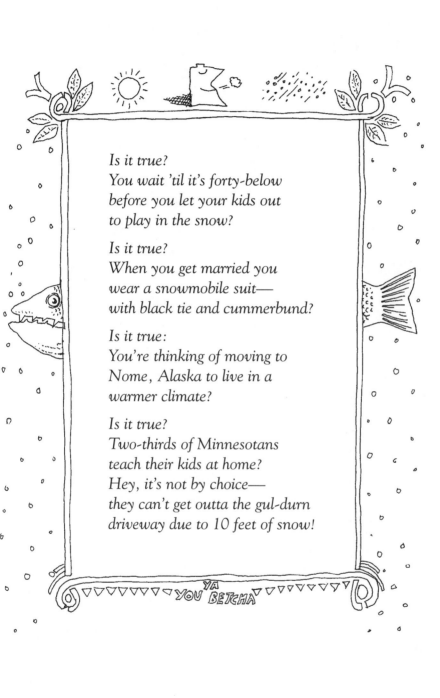

Is it true?
You wait 'til it's forty-below
before you let your kids out
to play in the snow?

Is it true?
When you get married you
wear a snowmobile suit—
with black tie and cummerbund?

Is it true:
You're thinking of moving to
Nome, Alaska to live in a
warmer climate?

Is it true?
Two-thirds of Minnesotans
teach their kids at home?
Hey, it's not by choice—
they can't get outta the gul-durn
driveway due to 10 feet of snow!

YA
YOU BETCHA

symphony and Duluth's symphony orchestras, plus the largest youth symphony program in the world. All in all, Twin Citians attend the arts at a rate twice the national average. Aren't you impressed?

"We're growing, growing, growing." (Or, everyone wants to live down here, not up there.)

Since when does *quantity* of life beat *quality* of life, anyway. Minnesota is the champ when it comes to quality of life. *Minnesota Heat* says so, and the myriad of independent studies on the matter confirm it. Not that this area is a slouch when it comes to out-and-out growth, either. Over the past decade, Minneapolis-St. Paul has been, and continues to be, the fastest growing major metropolitan area across the northern tier of the country—at a robust rate of 15.5% over the past decade. That's growth you can live with. Unemployment is well below the national average, income is well above it, and infrastruture keeps pace with it. Quality leads quantity in these parts—not the other way around. Ask yourself: What TV shows does "everyone" watch; and who watches the best shows on TV? Think about it.

"Now that you're (down) here, you can get rid of that sickly look."

How many times are you reminded about your "prison pallor" or otherwise baneful appearance at destinations south during winter? We know, we know—you desperately desire to be tan. It's glamorous, you "look better" and all that. But you should know, looks are often deceiving. Though they may pale, consider the consolations to palidity: Without year-round bronzing your skin doesn't age before you do—wrinkle, crinkle, leather, or compel a call to Michael Jackson's surgeon. Nor is the scary scan of the dermatologist so scary. Need you ask why skin conditions of a non-trivial nature are 15 times more prevalent in "healthy glow" country than they are up here?

Got a favorite *don't-let-'em-tell-ya?* Send it in. *Minnesota Heat* would like to know.

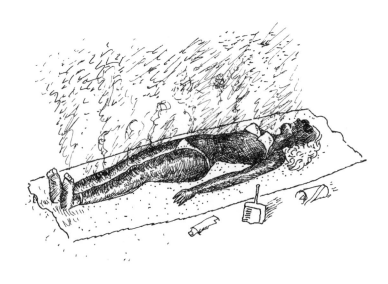

First Return Fire:
Showing a Little Initiative There

You've got to be especially careful with what we're getting into next: These are not just responses to the other guy's jabs—it's taking that fateful step beyond. You'd best go gingerly at first, lest you begin taking charge before you're ready for that mantle. Remember, too, even though your run-of-the-mill skulker has all that cliché bluster and put-down artistry at his command, he doesn't really know all that much about your environs when it comes right down to it, much less his own—not that's accurate, anyways. When you start spewing out hard information and using esoteric terms like Sun Sears and Dew Points, you'll be in danger of wresting the offensive away from him real quick. That's very unsettling to skulkers unaccustomed to descender status. And, are you ready to take on ascender status?

For starters, prudently use only enough of what you've collected from *Minnesota Heat* to this point, plus what you are about to learn in this chapter. This'll be enough to keep your tormentor off balance yet not prompt defensive epitaphs like: boring, peevish, jingoistic, insensitive, and wrongheaded—you know, all the things that *he* is. Use discretion.

Here we're going to get into some Minnesota firsts and things invented here. Firsts are particularly difficult for Minnesotans who are not comfortable with anything higher than second place. They come by this honestly—bestowed with some pretty high-profile second places in recent history. Like when the Minnesota Twins finished runners up to the Los Angeles Dodgers in the '65 World Series. Or like in the Stanley Cup finals when the Minnesota North Stars battled the New York Islanders in '83, and then the Pittsburgh Penguins in '91. Guess how those came out? And, how can any Minnesotan forget those historic performances by the Minnesota Vikings in Super Bowls IV, VIII, IX and XI? Second place was never in doubt.

On the political front, the legacy continues. Hubert Humphrey, from his number-two office of Vice President, came out number two against Richard Nixon in '68. And Walter Mondale, from his number-two office of Vice President, came out second to Ronald Reagan in '84. Remember Eugene McCarthy? And Harold Stassen? They were their party's solid runners-up right up to nomination.

Then in the very first quality-of-life study anyone can recall, by the prestigious Midwest Research Institute of Kansas City, Minnesota placed second among the 50 states. And lately? Well, Morgan Quintno Company's 1995 "State Rankings and State Perspectives" placed Minnesota as the second most livable state. But you guessed that, didn't you?

We're number two, Minnesotans dared to boast. Euphoria. But just when Minnesotans were proudly settling in with their second-place status, along came the cultural shocks of the '87 and '91 World Series. *Twins win!!* Minnesotans are still rebounding from the trauma of those upheavals.

Now, here comes *Minnesota Heat*, further traumatizing Minnesotans with still more firsts. Brace yourself.

Quality of Life. Relax. Minnesota is not always number one in these ratings. But out of the myriad of studies done on quality of life, Minnesota or one of its cities keeps popping up in the 1-5 slots in popular and professional journals. Funny thing: A surprising number of skulker habitats get passed over here. Hmmmm.

Softball. Well, kittenball, anyway, which became softball. It started at a Minneapolis fire station as a way to pass the time on 24-hour shifts, besides Checkers. A league eventually formed, the sport spread, a national organization unified rules, and softball caught fire to where it's become the number one participant team sport in the nation.

Water skiing. No, it wasn't the Florida Everglades—it was near Red Wing, Minnesota in 1922 that Ralph Samuelson strapped a couple of pine boards to his feet and, towed by an over-stressed outboard motor, skimmed across Lake Peppin. The rest is revisionist history.

Roller Blades. No, it wasn't California—it was St. Louis Park, Minnesota. In 1980, Brennan and Scott Olson had an idea they could extend the rinks to the streets. Now, in-line roller skating is on a roll across America.

Snowmobiles. No, not Canada—Roseau, Minnesota. Polaris Industries workers called them "iron dogs," as well they might. Today those dogs prowl 15,800 miles of snowmobile trails in Minnesota.

Let there be light. No, not the Great White Way—in 1882 the Minnesota Brush Electric Company converted the force of St. Anthony Falls into electric arc lighting for the city of Minneapolis. It was the first hydroelectric central station built in the United States.

Atlantic air crossing. Not *from* Minnesota—a *guy* from Minnesota. Charles Lindbergh was the first to do it. Lindy made the hop in 1927.

Indoor Regional Malls are all over the landscape now, but in 1956, there was only one—in Edina, Minnesota. Southdale was the first of four "Dales" soon to encircle the Twin Cities after that.

Mall of America is the first-of-its-kind mall in the U.S. It's located in Bloomington, Minnesota, if you just dropped in from Jupiter. It's 4.2 million square feet, with a seven-acre Camp Snoopy theme park in its midst. MOA has more annual visitors than Disney World and the Grand Canyon combined. And the doomsayers said it wouldn't work. (Of course, Minnesotans agreed with them. Heck, they *were* the doomsayers.)

Skyway walkways. The first skyways in the nation to connect buildings over street level, appeared in downtown Minneapolis in 1962. St. Paul unveiled its first skyway in 1967. Today, over 100 skyways link 94 city blocks in the Twin Cities. The system is immortalized by the Replacements, Minneapolis' well-known alternative band. *Skyway,* from the 1987 album *Pleased to Meet Me,* tells of a couple who may never meet because one takes the skyway and the other the street. Well, no one said skyways were perfect.

Automatic thermostats. Minneapolis Honeywell did us all a huge favor (back when it had a first name) by coming up with that little instrument in your hall. Sure, you're going to hear from your skulker friends: "It's because of the weather." (See Under the Weather. Nothing to Do.) When that happens, ask your friends from down there if they'd like to go without *their* thermostats when it's 110-degrees in the proverbial shade.

Radio jingles. The very first singing commercial aired in Minneapolis, with a male quartet intoning for one of General Mills' breakfast cereals: *"Have you tried Wheaties? They're whole wheat with all of the bran. Won't you try Wheaties? For Wheat is the best food of man."* That was over WCCO Radio, Christmas Eve, 1924. How time flies.

All puffed up. Speaking of breakfast cereals, the first cereal puffing process was invented in 1901 by a Minnesota college professor. From his invention, puffed wheat and puffed rice popped up on your table.

Medical Milestones. Breakthroughs here include open heart surgery, liver and pancreas transplants, iron-lung respirators, pacemakers and CT scans. The first certified nursing school was in Minnesota and HMO's first became health-care stars in the North Star State.

Smoking bans cleared the air first in Minnesota. Californians will claim it but Minnesotans did it. Smoke-free airline flights took off in Minnesota, too, via Northwest Airlines.

Scotch Tape. A company then named Minnesota Mining & Manufacturing came out with it, way back when.

Post-it Notes came some years later from the company now named 3M.

Magnetic recording tape reeled out somewhere between corporate name changes.

Northwest Airlines introduced the first closed-cabin commercial plane. Aren't you glad it caught on?

Corporate tithings. In the 1940's the Dayton Company began donating 5% of its pretax earnings to community educational institutions, the arts, and social services in Minnesota. In 1976 the nation's first Five Percent Club was formed with 23 companies pitching in. Now called the Keystone Program, firms from all over Minnesota have joined the club.

First on the dean's (and president's) list.
Minnesota ranks first in percentage of students graduated from high school, those going on to college, the ratio of its population in the workforce, and literacy. The state is commonly first in voter turnout for president, too, although you can't blame Minnesota for White House occupants—not enough electoral votes.

Tough Sledd'n. Adventurer/explorer Will Steger was the first to cross Antarctica by dog sled, in 1989-90. He was *not* trying to dramatize other places colder than his home town of Ely, Minnesota.

Treatment Centers. Try as you might, you're not going to find more dependency treatment centers than in these parts. Hazelden was the first of its kind in America. From that beginning the "Minnesota Model" spread across the nation.

Easy Livin'. Gallup interviews recently asked people to single out cities in their regions offering the best quality of life. Minneapolis was the Midwest winner. Guess even some skulkers out there know how to vote when it gets right down to it.

Recycling. Minneapolis was the first major city to have curbside pickup for recycling, which now has 90% participation. Minnesotans recycle 44% of their solid waste—more than any other state. No garbage.

First in Battle. The Minnesota First Volunteer Regiment was the first volunteer unit to join the Union armies at the outbreak of the Civil War. At Gettysburg, one of its companies prevented Union forces from being overrun when, with but 262 courageous men, outnumbered 20-1, they rushed past retreating Union forces straight into the advancing Confederates. They fired one volley before lowering their bayonets in a headlong final charge. And by God, they did it. They stopped the advance cold. Said Gen. Winfield Hancock, witness to it all:

> *"There is no more gallant deed recorded in history."*

On the following day, the Minnesota First threw itself against Pickett's Charge at the Union barricades, helping bring the bloody battle to its conclusion.

Be proud, Minnesotans.

We didn't mean to unnerve you with all these *firsts* and *number ones*, but we thought you should know. Take deep breaths. Maybe walk around the block. When you're ready, c'mon back. We've got some more good stuff for you.

Way up there's:

Now that we've broken the *number one* barrier (we have, haven't we?) let's deal with some other categories in which Minnesota ranks way up there.

Business and a whole lot more. When *Fortune* included living factors with its annual business evaluation of cities, Minneapolis placed number four on its 15 best-U.S.-cities rankings. Among things evaluated were crime, quality of schooling, availability of culture, state and local taxes (that should have taken care of the number-one slot)— right on down to the cost of a martini. Cheers.

Generation-X files. Now it seems Minneapolis is a hip place to be. *Swing*, a magazine for 20-somethings, named Minneapolis one of "The 10 Best Places to Live" for young people. It cites the area's music legacy (Prince, Soul Asylum, the Replacements, Hüsker Dü), parks, lakes, environment and plain ol' Minnesota nice. The magazine forgives coming up with blandities like Cream of Wheat.

ICE FISHING &
LISTENING TO
THE VIKINGS –
OR THE GOPHERS.

HAROLD L, OF DETROIT LAKES,
ENJOYING MINNESOTA'S QUALITY
OF LIFE.

City parks and such. Minneapolis maintains 170 park properties for parking yourself within its city limits. Approximately 11% of St. Paul is designated park land. Suburbs are extra.

Education. We've said it was high. Hey, it's even number one in some areas. Minnesota consistently ranks among the top three states in college entrance exams while regularly scoring 20 points above the national average. (Maybe this is why you're not communicating with skulkers all that well, Minnesotans.)

"Broadway," MN. Andrew Lloyd Weber's "Joseph and the Amazing Technicolor Dreamcoat" was boffo in Minneapolis before opening on Broadway. Same for "Victor/Victoria". And Disney's chose Minneapolis for it's pre-Broadway showing of "The Lion King", based largely on the success "Beauty and the Beast" had in the Twin Cities prior to opening on The Great White Way. Goes to show: Mickey really does love *Minne.*

"Hollywood," MN. Minnesota is a popular spot for making movies these days. You're likely familiar with the "Grumpy Old Men" and "The Mighty Ducks" series of films. And "Fargo". And Arnold Schwarzenegger's "Jingle All The Way". But are you aware "Equinox", "Little Big League", "The Heartbreak Kid", "Slaughter House Five", and

"Wild Rose" were all filmed in Minnesota? In 1995 alone, there were nine movies made in Minnesota including, "Feeling Minnesota", "Mallrats", "Portraits from the Cloth" and "Beautiful Girls". The trade paper *Hollywood Reporter* listed Minnesota as one of the five hottest—no sarcasm—locations for film making in North America.

... HE WAS TALL AND SORT OF TAN AND SMOKING A CIGAR ... AND WEARING A U.P.S. JACKET—BUT I FIGURED THAT WAS JUST A COVER!

AGAIN, AGNESS P. OF WAYZATA, MN "SPOTS" A CELEBRITY ... WHILE SHOPPING AT Byerly's

Runners' world. More Minnesotans participate in running than in any other sport. Three of the nation's top runs are the Twin Cities Marathon, Duluth's Grandma's Marathon and the Kaiser Roll 10K. Some 790 Minnesotans registered to run the Boston Marathon in 1996. Minnesotans have done all right in Bean Town. Fritz Carlson, a Minneapolis sawmill worker, won the Boston Marathon in 1913. Pine City's Dick Beardsley finished second to Alberto Salazar in 1982 by two seconds in what many consider the greatest closing duel in the marathon's history.

Fortune 500, and more. Dayton Hudson, 3M, Northwest Airlines, General Mills and Honeywell are among the 14 Minnesota companies on the Fortune 500 list of top U.S. publicly held companies in 1996—with two more companies on the bubble. Then there's Cargill, the largest privately owned company in the nation. Not too shabby for a state of only 4 1/2 million souls.

Wildlife. No, not that kind, the other kind— like in animals. Minnesota's wolf population (now cut that out) is the largest in the lower 48 states and is home to the only substantial population of timber wolves in the U.S. Also, Minnesota has the only sizable population of bald eagles in the U.S. other than Alaska. There are large herds of deer in the north woods, and all those Moose Lakes in Minnesota aren't just named for hat racks.

YOU NEVER HEARD OF MOOSE LAKE?

Publishing. Minnesota has the most concentrated printing and publishing industry in the United States and publishing has more presence in the Minnesota economy than in any other state. Minnesota ranks third in the nation for employment in book publishing behind only New York and California. How do you think *Minnesota Heat* got published?

You just have to face it: Minnesota *is* at the top of more than a few categories. Of course, the way you go about dispensing this information to skulkers is a tactical decision you'll have to make on your own. We recommend the time release method due to cultural disturbances a rapid-fire approach may agitate. It'll be easier on both you *and* your skulker friend when apportioned in measured dosages.

Minnesota Milestones:

Minnesota is progressing nicely forward according to *Minnesota Milestones*, the state's official report card for measuring long-term trends against established goals deemed important. Pretty darn progressive in itself when you think about it. Here's the outlook:

All Minnesotans will have a reasonable standard of living. Minnesotans are growing financially more secure, as measured by median family income trends which have exceeded the national level all along.

Minnesotans will have improved quality of air, water and earth. The number of days in violation of air quality standards is falling—it's now down to four.

Minnesota's environment will support a rich diversity of plant and animal life. The number of endangered, threatened or special-concern species is low and stable.

Minnesotans will have continued opportunity for enjoying the state's natural resources. Miles of recreational trails reach a whopping 21,000, and continue growing.

Minnesotans will provide stable environment for children. Juvenile drug use and apprehensions for other violations continue down, down, down.

Minnesota will have advanced education and training for meeting the global economy. University graduation rates are up, up, up.

Minnesotans will become healthier. That's good for the healthiest state around already, don't you think?

9 OUT OF TEN DOCTORS RECOMMEND MINNESOTA

We know this all starts to sound dangerously like boasting—and we feel your blanch. But hold on: The next chapter will help soothe your self-effacement birthright.

Give-backs:
Things to let up with.

I t helps to give back a little now and then, let up—once you get your skulker backpedaling. It aids your overall credibility, too, by acknowledging a few blemishes in the pristine tapestry you've begun to weave in front of him. And you'll feel better, as well. Minnesotans really take to this section.

Things you can complain about, while still boasting some:

Minnesota taxes. Here you admit you're worse off than he is (unless your skulker is from California or New York). But then you quickly add: "I get to deduct more punitive State Income Taxes against punitive Federal Income Taxes, than you get to do." Of course, the fact that you can actually *pay* those jolting Minnesota taxes won't be lost on your run-a-day skulker.

Long life (or does it just seem that way up here?). It's a fact Minnesotans *do* live longer than other Americans. "We probably keep better," you slip in, wryly. "Must be the weather," you coyly relinquish. Let 'em go contemplate.

Sin Laws. We're virtuous, you know. In Minnesota you can't enter a liquor store on Sundays, or get booze in a grocery store on *any* day. Liquor stores, where allowed, shut down at 8:00 p.m. on weekdays; bars close up tight at 1:00 a.m., including weekends. You should be home in bed.

Potholes. California motorists may have to brave rock slides on their highways now and again. Floridians have their road-eating sink holes to avoid on occasion. Arizonans are car-challenged with heaving pavement under the sun. All this is sissy stuff, you say, compared to the death-defying potholes Minnesota motorists face upon each winter's thaw. Kinda like sink holes filled with rocks between road heaves, you confess.

Home sweet home. The National Association of Homebuilders rates the Minneapolis metropolitan area as *most affordable* when it comes to buying a new home. Homes here are arguably *best built*, too. That's the boast part. It's the taxes you'll pay on your Minneapolis dream dwelling that'll bring you down a square foot or two. That's the concession part.

Dog Days. Perhaps Minnesota Nice extends to dogs. Most Minnesota dog owners won't admit to buying their pooch a Dairy Queen cone after a walk, but they know who they are. So why be surprised that "Dog Day Afternoon," an outdoor festival for canines, was bred in Minneapolis. Another way to spoil the top dog in the family, this tag-along festival features a "roll-in-fish pond," a pile of chewing shoes, a "doggy bone yard" and other fun and games for Bowser and Fifi. The Poodle Lounge serves "kitty-on-a-stick". And French cuisine, human style, is dog-dished up by a top French restaurant. Palate satisfied, Muffy pads over to Doggie Day Spa where her teeth are brushed, and her nails are clipped and polished. Pets can exchange "bow vows" at a Chapel, as well. Now, is this bragging or complaining? Or just plain embarrassing?

Out-and-out bad news, and other give-a-ways:

Bugs. Researchers say there are at least 8 million species of insects on the planet, of which only 1,085,000 have been discovered. Folks around here would think those researchers ought to look in Minnesota for the missing ones. Bugs can bug you in Minnesota but, even at that, they could be put in the *Don't-let-'em-tell-ya* chapter just as well as here. That's because, other states have their own infestations to contend with. While Minnesota is *wet*, June beetles, May beetles, gyspsy moths and most wood-boring insects love *dry.* Know any dry places? On the east coast black flies are all the rage. Florida has mosquitoes eclipsing even Minnesota's, plus fire ants—a lovely combination. Deer ticks just love New England. And California weather is wonderful for bugs of all kinds. At least Minnesotans only have to put up with most of their little blighters half the year. Winter has some benefits besides sleigh rides and skating rinks.

Mosquitoes. They're bugs, of course, but they rate a separate category all their own in Minnesota. More than 165 varieties of mosquitoes live in the USA, and Minnesotans are sure they all exist here. It's not that these pests can't be all but eliminated in the metropolitan area with a few more dollars per taxpayer, which the citizenry would gladly shell out for this purpose. But this is Minnesota, where legislators prefer hitting on constituents for social engineering projects and sundry behavioral ordinances instead. Minnesotans get stung both ways.

Liberal Lakes, Diversityville and Euphoria "townships". Joe Soucheray, Twin Cities radio talk-show host, calls attention to these enclaves of compassion and caring in Minnesota. Folks in these "communities" dutifully trust in the Tooth Fairy and have never seen a benevolently-packaged, feel-good government program they didn't hug to their bosom. Which leads to our next category.

Guilt and Taxes. Only social guilt weighs more heavily on Minnesotan shoulders than the tax burden they stagger under. One feeds the other, both spiraling ever upward. In Minnesota *guilt* and taxes are the first inevitabilities of human existence. Death comes later.

Minnesota politics. This is not to be believed, even by skulkers who would like to: Minnesota politicians at the outer extremes, Minnesota voters in the cozy middle, and never the twain shall meet. No one outside Minnesota can possibly conceive of the voids existing between these three disparate groups. But 'fess it up anyway, they'll think you're being gracious.

The Minnesota hunch. This stooped posture presents a lower profile to the elements, serving as a windbreak as well as a body-heat conservative. You might say it's a sort of Darwinian response to the less kinder days that will, once in a while, occur in Minnesota. Put another way: You don't adapt, you don't survive.

Chunk kicking. Here Minnesotans thrash wildly at the slushy collections of matter that adhere to their car fenders when winter conditions are just right. They do this with their feet, while taking care not to land prostrate in the street. The object is to bust each globule loose with one well-placed kick (or as few kicks as possible) bringing it down with a satisfying splat. This activity hits full stride during the warmer days of winter when it's easiest on shoe and toe, the chunks more readily let fly, and plop apart when they hit the asphalt. Is this great, or what?

Dreaded salt heel. Check those shoes come winter.

Morning jump start. Not caffeine, cables.

Ludefisk or lutefisk. You pick which one.

Minnesota drivers. As Charles Kuralt noted, "Minnesotans don't blow their horns behind you when the light turns green; they wait for you to notice." Unfortunately waiting for a Minnesota driver to notice can be a time consuming practice. So, too, is waiting for a Minnesotan to notice the stop sign is even there. Some Minnesotans obey speed limits diligently, while others ignore their exist-ence, totally. Those who heed them drive 20 miles *under* the limit as a margin of safety—in the left lane. Those who ignore them drive 20 miles *over* the limit—on the inside lane. All Minnesota motorists are gawkers, which tends to slow traffic a bit. A fender-bender on I-35W at rush hour results in a 10 o'clock News report of bumper-to-bumper traffic just breaking up.

Spine-chilling turns and jaw-dropping lane changes are routine. It's not that Minnesota drivers aren't courteous or considerate. They just don't know what they're doing out there.

Sunbelters do have a legitimate beef—what with Minnesota Snowbirds screwing up the normal flow of contentious bedlam on their thoroughfares four months out of the year.

THE WORST DAY IN MINNESOTA WINTER IS THE FIRST DAY IT SNOWS. EVERYBODY GOES: "WHAT'S THAT STUFF?" CRASH! "WHAT'S THAT STUFF?" CRASH! IT IS A RITUAL, LIKE BIRDS COMING BACK IN THE SPRING.

Minnesota Mindworks
and other inexplicables

S ome local behaviorism defies rational thought. We don't attempt to explain it, we just present it.

They go. They come back.

Some people move out of Minnesota (maybe even due to mental anguish brought on by skulkers) then, suddenly, they're back. It happens a lot. Yes, this State does fete you to longer winters than most. Yes, it's politically goofy much of the time. Yes, the taxes are borderline confiscatory. No, it's not the most friendly business locale you'll find. And, yes, there's a profusion of ordinances telling you how to live, act and breathe. But still, they're back. Maybe it's a form of return-migration, gleaned from waterfowl up here.

They *may* come. They *won't* go.

A recruiter from a prominent international executive search firm informed *Minnesota Heat* that the Twin Cities is one of the hardest areas to recruit *to*. But with those who have lived in the area for a couple of years (apparently Minnesota does require some acclimatizing), it's one of the three hardest areas in the United States to recruit *from*—all those weather ploys head hunters use not swaying them one scintilla. A national survey disclosed that Minnesota was at the bottom of the list of states to which business executives would want to relocate. But the same survey showed that once executives did locate here, it was harder to convince them to leave Minnesota than any other state in the country. Must be something in the water.

Refusing to show. Refusing to go.

Some years ago the Minnesota Vikings drafted a running back from Stanford as their number one pick. Darrin Nelson, a Californian through and through, refused to report. It's cold up there, he asserted, and, besides, there aren't enough discos. But the NFL reigns supreme, and "Disco Darrin" eventually signed with the Purple Gang. So where does Darrin make his family home now that his playing days are over? He is one of some 70% of former Vikings with a house on the prairie.

The Weather, She's-a-chang'n.

Ever have a skulker tell you how wonderful it is to have good weather all year round? "Good weather", in this instance, is understood to be unchangingly warm, even hot. But, is it really so? A study on weather and how it effects people showed that people are much more likely to be psychologically bothered and depressed by *unchanging* weather than by *changing* weather. If that's true, Minnesotans, you're living in mental Nirvana.

Honk if you like Minnesota.

They crowd golf courses, stroll the parks in great numbers, lounge on public beaches as if they owned them, cut across lawns and make a lot of noise. No, they're not raucous neighbors—not people neighbors, anyhow. They're geese. Two-hundred thousand breeding Canada Geese reside in Minnesota, including about 25,000 in the Twin Cities, where they numbered only 1,000 a few years back. Bird directories from not long ago show Canada Geese habitats broaching only the northern tip of Minnesota. Those days have flown as the big birds have feathered new nests. Efforts over the past several years to trap and release the large flyers in neighboring states have largely failed. Why? Like many people leaving Minnesota, they come home to roost.

A solution to getting goosed is to harvest some of the fowl and donate their meat to Food Shelves for the disadvantaged. Seems simple enough, but the idea neither floats nor flies well in Minnesota. You see, animal rights persons are as plentiful as geese around here, and they can squawk just as loudly. Surfacing next on the animal rights agenda, we're told, is a call to scale back on fishing. Just how will resident fisherpersons react to *that*? Now there's a *real* Minnesota polarization of mind-sets for you. Keep a gander on that one.

Land O'Water

Minnesotans are awash in lakes. Is there a native Minnesotan who doesn't know how to swim, who hasn't fished, water skied, gone boating or spent time at a lake cabin? Minnesota lake life is so pervasive that even skulkers are fascinated by its magnitude. *Minnesota Heat's* advice? Talk up lakes next time skulkers are trying to sink you. You might even find them listening for a change. Lakes have an attraction for everyone—even *them.*

When the last glaciers receded 11,000 years ago they left water behind. Lots of water. Right today there are 15,291 bodies of water large enough to be classified as lakes in Minnesota. More lakes than in any other state. More than 90,000 miles of shoreline. Seven-thousand, seven-hundred and sixty-two square miles of lakes, not counting ponds and wetlands, or the 25,000 miles of rivers and streams of which the mighty Mississippi is one. And it doesn't cover the 200 miles bordering on the mother of all freshwater bodies: Lake Superior. There are lakes in all but one of Minnesota's 87 counties. There are 200 cities and towns in Minnesota named for lakes, bays, beaches, rapids, falls, rivers, creeks or just plain water. Minneapolis alone has chains of lakes, singular lakes, streams, ponds, waterfalls, and rivers running through it.

Up to the Lake.

Lake country in Minnesota starts in earnest in the center of the state, continuing northward into the Arrowhead region which meets Lake Superior on its north shore. We're talking serious laking here. Sixty percent of all Minnesota households head out to lake homes or resorts sometime during the year—owned rented or borrowed. It's estimated that 15,000 Twin Cities residents at any given moment are looking for a lake place to buy. When Minnesotans go to *a* lake, it's called *the* lake. What lake that is, out of the thousands of possibilities, is left for you to somehow divine. More completely, the statement usually goes, "We're going *up to the lake*." That's because some 54% of Minnesotans live in the Minneapolis-St. Paul area to the south, so going to the lake is *up*. (It's, "We're going *out* to the lake," for the Minnesotans more northernly situated.)

Up to the lake in Minnesota has been defined as: *A migratory pattern, usually occurring on Friday*

HARVEY H. OF KENWOOD, MN HAS DECIDED HE WILL
COUNT MINNESOTA'S "10,000 LAKES."

afternoons during the summer, distinguished by over-loaded vehicles of absorbing sorts, boat trailers and a homing instinct for knotty pine. Would we kid you? Not on your life. The Minnesota History Center posts just such a definition. Now's that fascinating to skulkers, or not?

Minnesotans take to the lakes in the winter, too, when they're not fleeing south. They tow little huts out onto the lake, drill holes through the ice and fish for the big ones that got away during summer. Some lakes actually become small villages of ice-fishing houses. There may even be a card game, or a nip or two on occasion in these cozy decked-out lilliputan lake homes while waiting for the wily walleye to strike. It's hard to know for sure. Lake Mille Lacs, a veritable walleye factory with over half a million pounds of walleye pike taken annually, has fishermen laying out streets and avenues among the "village's" 5,000 huts atop the frozen surface of the lake—housing a population of some 25,000 enthusiasts.

With water splashing all around, it shouldn't come as any real surprise that Minnesota hosts one watercraft for every six residents. Minnesota ranks first nationally in sales of fishing licenses per capita, and is number one outright in outboard motor sales and ownership. Only Michigan has more boats over all than Minnesota.

Rivers are tributary to Minnesota's vast water acreage. Rivers flow out of Minnesota north to

Hudson Bay, east to the Atlantic Ocean and south to the Gulf of Mexico. The Minnesota River was once larger than the Mississippi when fed by retreating glaciers. The St. Croix River is one of the most beautiful flowages in the world, its upper reaches protected as a wilderness area. Between rivers, lakes and streams, wanna guess how much of this state is under water?

Up the River.

At its source (Lake Itasca, for aliens) you can cross the soon-to-be mighty Mississippi by gingerly traipsing over rocks from one "bank" to the other. You'd think this spot would have been discovered by explorers of the Minnesota territory, early on. You just follow that there big river upstream 'til you do, right? But this seemingly simple task eluded Europeans and frontier Americans for more than 200 years starting way back in the 1620's. Their efforts ended with the discovery, instead, of difficult rapids, other harsh conditions and wrong turns into numerous tributaries. Father Louis Hennepin set out to find the illusive source after becoming the first European to lay eyes on the falls he named St. Anthony, in 1680—the eventual birth site of Minneapolis. The Sioux had other ideas, though. It wasn't until 1832 that a little known writer named Henry Schoolcraft, accompanied by an Indian guide known as Yellow Head, finally found and identified the river's true source. Schoolcraft merged the Latin word "veritas" meaning *true*, and "caput" meaning *head*, to form the word: Itasca. And you thought Itasca was an Indian name.

So there you have it. A long way a-winding, but *Minnesota Heat* thought you should know that there. Skulkers, too.

Unsolved mystery.

It took 200 years to solve *that* Minnesota river riddle. We still haven't solved another: The mystery of Devil's Kettle.

The Brule River is one of 33 Minnesota rivers that flows into Lake Superior. As the river bends on its rush toward the great lake, a bedrock knob splits its waters sending half cascading over a waterfall into a great pool canyoned by vertical walls up to sixty feet high, and half into a great circular cauldron: Devil's Kettle. Dramatic! But the thing is, the half of the Brule that drops into Devil's Kettle just disappears. Could it be the water lunges into a great lava tube, to be dispelled somewhere beneath the surface of Lake Superior? These are all volcanic rocks around here, are they not? Trouble is, geologists say, they're not the right kind of volcanic rocks to form tunnels. And no lava tubes have ever been found in the hundreds of lava flows along the North Shore. Nor have there been any reports of trees or other floating debris suddenly appearing at any one spot off Lake Superior's shore such as an underground river might produce. Nor are there any backwaters or pooling points in the area.

So, we're left with half of a raging river just vanishing before our eyes without a geological clue. Give the Devil's Canyon its due.

Fish Stories.

With water come fish. And with fish come an-glers. And with anglers come stories. Big stories. A sign over President Herbert Hoover's fishing lodge once read: *Lord, suffer me to catch a fish so large that even I in talking of it afterward shall have no need to lie.* It's not that Minnesotans actually lie about the fish they catch, or those that got away—stretching the truth (and the fish) would be a kinder way of putting it.

Minnesotans can even match out-of-state skulkers with boasts when it comes to their beloved fish tales. What might be the record Minnesota fish story of all, though, now stands as a Minnesota record. In 1929, a man named J. V. Schanken allegedly caught a northern pike in Basswood Lake, near Ely, Minnesota, which is officially registered as the biggest one ever caught in the state: 45 pounds, 12 ounces. Minnesota's legacy of outsized fish, and anglers catching them, is well documented, but this one smells a little fishy. No one by the name J. V. Schanken was ever born or has ever died in Minnesota according to state records. No one has the name Schanken now living in Minne-sota, either. Nor did *The Ely Miner,* the area newspaper at the time, carry a mention of such a monster fish, although it carried stories that same year of a 22 1/2-pound lake trout caught by famed Minnesota wilderness advocate Sigurd Olson, and a 32-pound lake trout caught by another fortunate angler, taken in the vicinity. It's not that Basswood Lake isn't capable of

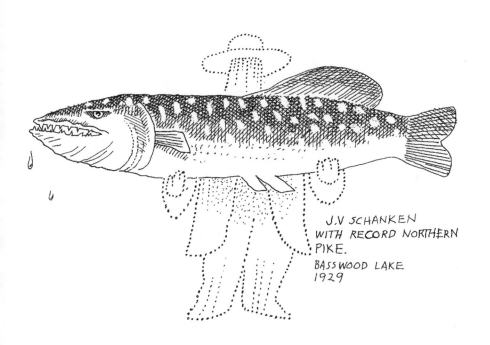

J.V SCHANKEN
WITH RECORD NORTHERN
PIKE.
BASSWOOD LAKE
1929

producing northerns in the 40-pound class, but it does raise the question: Is this "45-12er" Minnesota's ultimate fish story?

Far be it for *Minnesota Heat* to suggest it, but couldn't J. V. Schanken serve as an inspirational role model for Minnesotans dealing with Geo-climatic Skulkers?

Underwater World.

As if Minnesota didn't have enough water, it also harbors the largest aquarium of its type in the nation.

Deep under the Mall of America, Underwater World takes you on a journey to Poseidon. You begin in a Boundary Waters setting of late fall. Trout streams are running, loon calls cry out and forest smells and northern lake fog hang in the air.

You leave the forest through a clear tunnel that leads under a typical northern Minnesota lake surround where native species of Minnesota fish ply the waters. You see muskies, northern pike, walleye and yellow perch like you never landed. Then you're at the bottom of the Mississippi River with its natural inhabitants swimming about—catfish, bluegills, six-foot alligator gars, and flatheads. Next you pass under the Gulf of Mexico replete with species of shark, diamond rays and red drums. Finally, you reach a coral reef populated with colorful, exotic sea citizenry.

In all, you're immersed among 25,000 under-water creatures large and small.

Where else can you have a like experience? You could travel to New Zealand where there's a similar aquarium. And there's an underwater world aquarium in San Francisco, although quite a bit smaller. So, where ya gonna go?

Down South.

I n Minnesota, if it's not *up north* it's *down
south* when retreating from the confines of
the Twin Cities metropolitan area—if the
"Cities" can be considered confining. "To seek a
reprieve from the noise and haste amid rolling
fields of corn and alfalfa rather than in shadowy
woodlands, and without a substantial lake within
fifty miles—this, in a Minnesotan, is almost the
stuff of cultural subversion," writes D. J. Tice in
Mpls. St. Paul Magazine. Scribed columnist John
Torgrimson, in the *Fillmore County Journal:* "It's
your own damn fault if you're stressed out in
Fillmore County," which is where we're talking
about in southeastern Minnesota.

This is bluff country Minnesota with a tranquillity
all its own. The scenery is painted with clear-
rushing streams, high ridges, deep-cut ravines,
and hills and valleys, washed in colors of sea-

sonal pallet rolling out to distance. Fish the streams, hike and bike the trails, hunt the fields or just laze and gaze. It's land to savor.

No big-city machinations hereabouts. Consider Whalan, Minnesota, residing in a gorge of the Root River flowing through Fillmore County. Whalan drew some note when it held a Stand Still Parade. What's a Stand Still Parade? Well, Whalan didn't figure it was big enough for a regular type parade. So the floats, convertibles, bands, beauty queens, and all, just stood still. After all, there was no place to go but out of town. The "crowd" (those left over from the town's 90 residents and any outsiders who happened through at the time) then milled about, taking in the pageantry propped immobile before them. It was a moving experience, we're told—for the viewers, at least. It just might be, too, that Whalan has given us yet another Minnesota *first* to chalk up.

"Fargo."

G ot time for a movie break?

Fargo isn't in Minnesota, it's across the border in North Dakota. Nevertheless, the movie by this title is about Minnesota, set in Minneapolis and Brainerd up there in lake country. Surprisingly, some of the same Minnesotans who let skulkers beat them up without a whimper get disordered with this movie's joshings. *Minnesota Heat's* view of the film is more favoring:

> Minnesotans aren't the evil ones in this movie—they infiltrate from beyond these borders. And it's the bad guys from elsewhere that use those nasty words and do all that messy violence. The Minnesota plotter really doesn't know what it takes to be honest-to-gosh bad—it's why his scheme is so naive, and destined to go wrong from the

start. The Minnesota businessmen are honorable for the better part. The Minnesota male lonely-heart hasn't the heart to follow through with his clumsy proposition. The Minnesota prostitutes aren't hard-bitten souls, either—they're even polite. Margie, the Minnesota cop is honesty, integrity and compassion personified. Her plaintive soliloquy wraps up "Fargo's" tragic story—the contrasting presence of the surviving evil-doer making her words all the more poignant:

> *"Insanity in Brainerd. And for what? For a little bit of money. (pause) There's more to life than money don't y'know? (pause) And here we are. (long pause, tears welling) And it's such a beautiful day."*

OK, the Coen brothers might have gone lighter on the "Ya-ahs" in the film. But the only real question *Minnesota Heat* has about "Fargo" is: Who found all that money, come warm weather?

Under the Weather.
Nothing to Do.

N ow let's deal with two pincers skulkers will use on you whenever you offer any thing positive about Minnesota in con-versation. You'll need to stand your ground as well as The Minnesota First at Gettysburg when meeting with these two ploys: The *It's because of the weather* and/or the *There's nothing else to do,* answers to everything you have to say about Minnesota.

Know that your hard-core antagonists will em-ploy these techniques unblushingly.

OK now. Turn the page.

The *Because of the Weather* answer to everything:

You say: "The very first enclosed mall was built in Edina, Minnesota."

They say: "It's because of the weather."

You say: "A nice thing about Minneapolis is the Skyway system connecting its buildings, downtown."

They say: "It's because of the weather."

You say: "Much of the Minnesota Zoo is climate-controlled. And there's an enclosed monorail for touring natural habitats outside."

They say: "It's because of the weather."

You say: "Minneapolis has more theater groups per capita than any other city in the nation."

They say: "It's because of the weather."

You say: "Minnesota is a flourishing medical center—with the highest percentage of managed care coverage in the country."

They say: "It's because of the weather."

You say: "Minnesotans read a lot, having the highest literacy rate in the U.S."

They say: "It's because of the weather."

You say: "Carry-out boys bring your groceries to your car for you."
They say: "It's because of the weather."

You say: "I haven't been feeling well."
They say: "It's because of the weather."

You say: "The Mall of America has the largest enclosed theme park in the world."
They say: "It's because of the weather."

You say: (talking about the Twin Cities' leading-edge role in the coffee-shop phenomenon as it ground through the nation):
"There's a shop on every corner."
They say: "It's because of the weather."

You say: "I've got to go to the bathroom."
They say: "It's because of the weather."

The "*There's nothing else to do*" answer to everything else:

You say: "The Minnesota Timberwolves hold the NBA season attendance record."
They say: "There's nothing else to do."

You say: "The Twin Cities broke all attendance records for the Smithsonian Traveling Exhibit, and it was held over for the first time, anywhere.
They say: "There's nothing else to do."

You say: "More fishing licenses are issued in Minnesota than in any other state."

They say: "There's nothing else to do."

You say: "More hunting licenses are issued in Minnesota than in any other state."

They say: "There's nothing else to do."

You say: "Record breaking crowds attended the U.S. Open here.

They say: "There's nothing else to do."

You say: "Parks [all over the place] are really popular in Minnesota."

They say: "There's nothing else to do."

You say: "Minnesota normally has the highest voter turnout in the nation."

They say: "There's nothing else to do."

You say: "Minnesota recycles more solid waste material than any other state."

They say: "There's nothing else to do."

You say: "Duck hunting gets big billing in Minnesota."

They say: "There's nothing else to do."

You say: "Water sports make a big splash in Minnesota."

They say: "There's nothing else to do."

SKULKER VIEW OF OUTDOOR
RECREATION IN MINNESOTA.

You say: "There are hiking trails, biking paths,
            running paths, cross-country ski
            trails, groomed snowmobile runs and
            downhill ski areas all across the
            state."
They say: "There's nothing else to do."

These tactics are interchangeable in some cases.
And when both are leveled at a single statement
made by you, recognize you're faced with an
unmitigated skulker of the worst sort. So, what
to do?

The *There's nothing else to do,* answer to everything is the easiest of the two to deal with in
most instances. Keep heaping on Minnesota
activities until your antagonist gets it through
his baked brain that repeating "There's nothing
else to do," to the 50th activity you bring up
contradicts even a Geo-climatic Skulker's logic.

This is when your skulker friend may shift to,
It's because of the weather—a tougher premise
to deal with. The weather *does* have a little to do
with Minnesotans having more indoor tennis
courts. And the weather *does* have something to
do with the Hubert H. Humphrey Metrodome's
mushroom stance in downtown Minneapolis.

So, if you can't fight 'em, join 'em. Or, rather,
have *'em* join *you*—as has been happening,
when you think about it:

    More than a few more climate-controlled
    malls have made their appearance since

IT WAS KEVIN'S FIRST TIME DEER HUNTING.
YOU WOULD NOT BE REMISS IF YOU SAID
HE HAS A LOT TO LEARN.

Southdale made its, wouldn't you say? (Kind of nice, shopping away from the elements.)

Enclosed skyways are being studied and emulated by cities elsewhere. (Kind of nice, strolling in climate-controlled comfort out of street traffic.)

Enclosed theme parks are in the planning stages at several locales outside of Minnesota. (Kind of nice watching the kiddies enjoy themselves in air-conditioned solace.)

Domed tennis courts are mushrooming up all over the land. (Kind of nice enjoying the game year round under controlled conditions.)

More and more zoos around the country are using climate-controlled enclosures to simulate the natural environments of resident animals. (Kind of nice observing the beasties going about their business in their native climates provided.)

Domed stadiums are not just for cold climates, now are they? (Houston, do we have a problem?)

And next time you hear that rap about the weather putting you under it, just remember Minnesota is number one on health insurance charts. And, only Hawaiians have a longer average life span than Minnesotans. Maybe it *is* the weather.

All this may be a little more confrontational than Minnesota Nice allows for you. So we won't hold it against you if you bow out at this juncture. You've given it a shot coming this far. At least you can take solace in the fact that you're a more *aware* Minnesotan now than before, conscious of how skulkers operate. Maybe that's enough. But you've traveled this distance. It seems a shame to give it up now. Victory is at hand. Give us yours.

IN MINNESOTA WE HUNT, FISH, SKI, SKATE, SWIM, BIKE, BOAT, PICNIC, HIKE, WATER SKI, GOLF, PLAY TENNIS, LOVE SPORTS EVENTS, GO TO PLAYS AND CONCERTS — OH YEAH...WE READ A LOT, TOO.

THERE'S NOTHING ELSE TO DO.

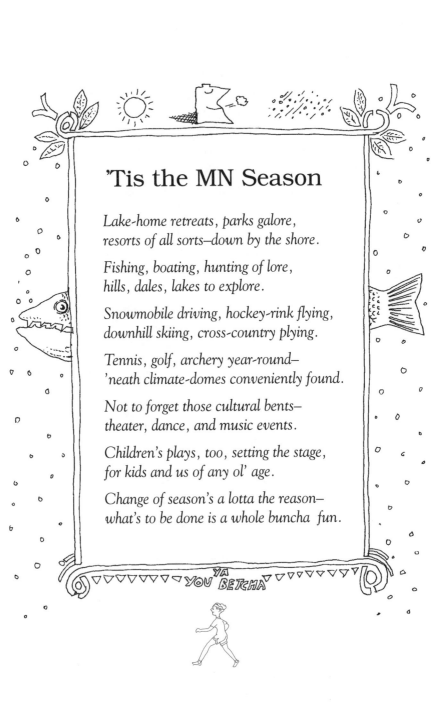

'Tis the MN Season

Lake-home retreats, parks galore,
resorts of all sorts—down by the shore.

Fishing, boating, hunting of lore,
hills, dales, lakes to explore.

Snowmobile driving, hockey-rink flying,
downhill skiing, cross-country plying.

Tennis, golf, archery year-round—
'neath climate-domes conveniently found.

Not to forget those cultural bents—
theater, dance, and music events.

Children's plays, too, setting the stage,
for kids and us of any ol' age.

Change of season's a lotta the reason—
what's to be done is a whole buncha fun.

YA YOU BETCHA

War of Attrition.

A particular talent of Geo-climatic Skulkers is that they can *disremember* anything of a positive nature you bring up about Minnesota within minutes. This makes it doubly hard for you when you *can't* forget the bombasts coming from the other direction, while trying your darndest.

It's exhausting. It's wearing. It's frustrating. You've offered up umpteen informational gems culled from *Minnesota Heat* with little or no take. When this happens, you know you're in a war of attrition—it often comes to that with these die-hard skulkers who'd make Bruce Willis look like a quitter. That's when its time for *attrition trivia*—not much of substance perhaps but neither is anything your skulker friend has likely offered up. Besides, it's kind of fun stuff. Just remember, we're into attrition now, not content. Not that your skulker will likely notice the difference.

Attrition Trivia:

- Minnesota is the twelfth largest state by area, with 84,068 square miles.

- Minnesota has 56 state forests, three national forests and 33 state wildlife centers.

- There are more than 6,000 campsites in Minnesota.

- Minnesota is number one in homes with phones. (Because of the weather?)

- There are 24 art museums and science centers in Minnesota.

- Minnesota is number one in sweet corn (sorry Iowa), sugar beets, turkeys (you knew that) and non-fat dry milk (yuck).

- St. Paul was originally named Pig's Eye after the Canadian Voyageur (and bootlegger), Pig's Eye Parrant, who first established the community. Father Galtier came along a few years later and renamed the settlement after his patron saint, Paul. Today Pig's Eye is a St. Paul beer, Galtier is a St. Paul plaza and St. Paul is a capital city.

- Minneapolis was St. Anthony before it became Minneapolis. Its name comes from *minne,* the Dakota Indian word for water, and *polis,* the Greek word for city—chosen after city fathers decided that two cities across the river from each other, both named for saints, weren't compatible. Some think they aren't, still.

- Minnesota blends *minne,* water, with the Dakota word *sota,* for sky. A translation is, land of sky blue waters.

- Duluth, on Lake Superior, is the largest fresh water port in the world—2300 nautical-miles from the Atlantic Ocean. More shipping tonnage moves through Duluth than any other port in the country except New York.

- More than half the cake mixes in the U.S. come from Minneapolis where Betty Crocker and the Pillsbury Doughboy are alive, well and dwell.

- The blueberry is the state muffin. Milk is the state drink. The morel is the state mushroom. Wild rice is the state grain. Walleye is the state fish. Gophers and loons are state-bequeathed, too, but not on any state menus you can bet.

- The Sawtooth Range along the north shore of Lake Superior comprises the oldest mountains in North America.

- A billion years ago lava began spewing through the Earth's crust near what is now Minnesota's North Shore. After a few million years of eruptions the crust sank, forming a basin. The Ice Age came along next, gouging the basin for a few hundred-thousand more years. As the glaciers retreated for the last time, Lake Duluth grew into Lake Minong-Houghton, which grew into Nipissing, which grew into Lake Superior.

- Lake Superior is so large it has measurable tides. The water it contains could cover Canada, the United States and South America to a depth of one foot.

- Eagle Mountain is Minnesota's highest point at 2301 feet above sea level. It's only a flint-stone's throw from there to Minnesota's lowest point, 602 feet above sea level, on the Lake Superior shore.

- The Red River Valley in northwest Minnesota is the residual of Lake Agassiz, a post glacial body of water that was once larger than all the Great Lakes combined.

- Upper and Lower Red Lakes are the largest fresh water bodies within the borders of any state.

- Mesabi (Hibbing's largest open mine pit in the world) means giant. So does Paul Bunyan in these parts, as well as does Le Sueur Valley's Jolly Green Ho-Ho-Ho'er.

- Statues of Paul Bunyan stand tall in Bemidji and Brainerd. Both towns claim him. The guy's big enough for both.

- The Paul Bunyan Trail stretches 100 miles from Brainerd to Bemidji, touching 12 lake communities as it meanders past lakes and through forests. It's a paved paradise for hikers, cyclists, in-line skaters, snowmobilers and cross-country skiers. A trek worthy of Paul.

- "A proper snow is worth a pile of manure," says an old French proverb. A snow blanket absorbs nitrates, calcium, potassium, and sulfate—then makes like a time-release capsule for the soil. A generous snowfall is good news to Minnesota farmers.

- Minnesota is four-hundred and six miles north to south—more than 25% of the distance between Hudson's Bay and the Gulf of Mexico. It's "little chimney," resulting from a mapmaker's mistake, is the most northerly point of the United States. But for that miscue Maine might well be taking all that Minnesota heat today.

- The Boundary Waters Canoe Area is the largest federal wilderness east of the Rockies. Don't leave camp without a compass.

- The original Mayo Clinic is in Rochester. You see it on TV whenever the parade of national and international celebrities and dignitaries drop in for a check-up.

- "Grumpy Old Men" introduced you to Wabasha, Minnesota. Or was it Hastings? Or St. Paul? Or Stillwater? Or all of the above? A little filmatic license, there.

- The world's largest statute of a pelican resides in, where else, Pelican Rapids, Minnesota.

- The world's largest prairie chicken (grouse to some) rousts in Rothsay, Minnesota. It weighs 4 1/2 tons. It'll never fly.

- Darwin, Minnesota is listed in the *Guinness Book of Records*, for having the world's largest ball of string. There's a twist for you.

- Remember Christian Bros. Hockey Sticks mentioned earlier? Guess what's proudly displayed outside of corporate headquarters in Warroad, Minnesota. Ya betcha: the world's largest hockey stick.

- Land of Swedes and Norwegians? Maybe so, but there are more Germans nesting in Minnesota than all Scandinavians combined—including Finlanders, fer sure. And would you guess it? Minnesota has the largest Hmong population in the nation.

- Speaking of Norwegians, Viking explorers left what's known as The Kensington Runestone near Alexandria, Minnesota more than 100 years before Columbus became a hot-shot explorer. Discovered in 1898 by a Swedish-immigrant farmer, the 200 pound stone has been translated to read:

> *"8 Goths and 22 Norwegians on exploration journey from Vinland over the west We had come by skerries on day journey north from this stone We were and fished one day After we came home found 10 men red with blood and dead Ave Maria save from evil Have 10 of our party by the sea to look after our ships 14 days journey from this island Year 1362"*

The least we could do is name a Minnesota football team for those brave souls.

• Do you know what Mississippi stands for, besides being a tough word to spell? It's the Algonquin Indian word for *great river*. The Algonquins had it right—it's the third greatest river in the world, journeying 2,552 miles from Minnesota to the Gulf of Mexico.

• Jesse James and his gang got chased out of Northfield, Minnesota, his first rout as a bank robber. Jesse's gang was never the same after that—or as many. Minnesotans know how to hunt and shoot.

• The IDS Tower, First Bank Tower and Norwest Tower, the three tallest buildings in Minneapolis, all stand within 2 1/2 vertical feet of each other. Norwest deferred to the IDS Tower (Minneapolis' tallest), when it erected its building. It would have been "gauche" to make it the city's tallest building, its architect said of his tower. So did First Bank avoid unthinkable gaucherie when it built its new tower a bit later. But guess what? It peaks above banking rival Norwest, while stopping just short of IDS's elevation. Now that's *Minnesotan.*

As we said earlier, your most ardent skulkers will clear their minds of what you've hit them with here, almost as fast as you deliver it. That being the case, you can recite the same list over again and hold the initiative. With craniums emptied, they won't recognize your trivia roll-overs for what they are.

Star-studded Trivia:

For variety, you can also drop some Minnesota born celebrity names on them. They'll be dumb-founded. No skulker thinks anyone noteworthy comes from Minnesota. And a big advantage you'll have here is that skulkers can't resist *noteworthies,* especially noteworthies with *celeb-rity-glitz* attached to them. The entertainer formerly known as Prince, is a native, and makes his home in Minnesota. Same with Leo Kottke. Academy Award winner, Jessica Lange, still has a home in Minnesota. And, guess where Judy Garland, Bob Dylan and Roger Maris all hail from? Hey man, here.

Your Quick-Scan Traveler coming up combines a copious list of Minnesota home-grown celebs along with other handy rapid-reads for skulkers

retaliation. Skulkers will likely recognize the entertainers and jocks, although they may have trouble with the authors and other learned ones. Except for Charles Schulz, of Peanuts fame, you may have to rely on the fact that Sinclair Lewis, Harrison Salisbury and F. Scott Fitzgerald have names with an important ring to them. Don't expect skulkers to recognize authors just because they're accomplished. Same with other fields of endeavor: U.S Supreme Court justices, for instance. Trot out these distinguished names anyway, your skulker friends just might pretend to know who you're talking about.

One name, with a lot of punch, you should be aware of as we go forward is the redoubtable crusader, Captain Marvel—created, written and illustrated by Minnesota's C. C. Beck. What better role model is there for you than this legendary super hero? SHAZAM! You're transformed.

Now, a final flight check before you go soaring up, up, and away.

Minnesota Wraps

I f you've faithfully followed *Minnesota Heat* guidelines to this point, you've surely made major head way toward becoming a new and bolder Minnesotan. Congratulations.

Some of you, though, may still lean toward life as you've always known it rather than taking up the cudgel against all those skulkers out there. The intractability. The obstinacy. The obtuseness. It's too much to fight, some may conclude.

Even so, you'll find you can't go all the way back after your exposure to *Minnesota Heat*—that you've gained self image and inner peace you didn't possess before. You've picked up on things, become a more aware person. Skulkers will sense there's something different about you—that you're no longer the Minnesotan they once knew, counted on, coveted.

Skulkers don't want to know what they don't know, as you now know. And now that *you* know that, even the most hide-bound skulker will at least *suspect* you know that. So whatever ragging you get from here on out will not have the same sting as before—not as delivered, not as received. Perhaps that's enough recompense for you. Besides, you may ask, what are skulkers going to jabber on about once you shut 'em down on Minnesota? Certainly not Plato. They'll be dispossessed of a favorite pastime. And just maybe, *there's nothing else for them to do!*

Final preps for the courageous.

If you're prepared to take things all the way against your out-of-state haranguers, we applaud you. But before raging on, we offer these words of restraint (if issuing words of restraint to Minnesotans isn't akin to carrying coals to Newcastle). It's a final five-point check before venturing south with your new-found confidence.

1. There's a big difference between being assertive and being aggressive. Don't overdo it. Of course, you've got to get to assertive first.

2. Focus your response so as not to get flustered. Do deep breathing and practice in front of a mirror. Speaking into a tape recorder can help, if you can get used to that weird accent playing back at you.

MINNESOTANS! DON'T STAND
THERE AND TAKE IT ANYMORE.
FIGHT BACK, IN THE
NAME OF PAUL BUNYAN
AND HUBERT HUMPHREY

SAY ANYTHING! IF IT ISN'T WITTY,
MAKE IT OUTRAGEOUS. OUTRAGEOUS!
"HEY! BIG JIM, I DIDN'T RECOGNIZE
YOU WITHOUT YOUR "SMOG/RADIATION
JACKET."

3. Make eye contact when you speak. It's best to avoid the Minnesota inclination to trace zigzag patterns on the ground with your foot while attempting to make a point.

4. If your skulker friend resists your best efforts and attempts to regain the initative, appear to listen intently while taking time to untangle your tongue before responding. A rejoinder from *Minnesota Heat* will surely come to mind if you stall long enough. Here you *might* try tracing your foot around on the ground.

5. Reflect on how you did. What worked. What didn't. Don't despair if you don't get it right the first few times you try. Standing up for one's self is unfamiliar territory for most Minnesotans. Remember, Geo-climatic Skulkers will give you ample opportunity for practice. Of course, you know that.

At last, you're ready. Just keep in mind what *Minnesota Heat* has taught you. Use your handy Quick-scan Travelor, coming up next. And arm yourself with *Minnesota Heat Take-alongs* offered at the back of the book.

Bon Voyage, good luck, and remember your trivia.

Minnesota Heat
Quick-scan Traveler

When confronted, shoot from the hip (pocket).

To assist you against skulkers, we offer an invaluable fight-back tool. It's the *Minnesota Heat Quick-scan Traveler,* loaded for rapid-fire retaliation. Carry it with you at all times. Once brandished (and recognized for what it is), you may not even have to fire off a single salvo. Seeing you're armed this way, bushwhackers will scurry for cover faster than in a Clint Eastwood bar scene, if they know what's good for them. All those skulkers will be forced to turn to less fortunates than yourself. Why, you might even feel bad about spoiling their fun for a fleeting moment—a Minnesota Nice sort of tenet. But better their fun than yours, don't you think?

Yes, with *Minnesota Heat*, its *Quick-scan Traveler* (plus *Take-alongs* you can order from the last chapter), you'll be a Minnesota arrival who's finally *arrived.* No more Minnesota heat. Cool!

Debunking bunk

Bunk

Debunk

"It's not the heat, it's the humidity."

There's more than meets the skin, here, Crusty. In addition to ambient temperature and humidity, your comfort is effected by breeze (a body-heat take-away) and Sun Sear (a body-heat add-on). The farther south you go, the greater the Sun Sear add-on. Forget the humidity—dive for the shade, and catch a breeze if you can. Warning: Lack of humidity can be hazardous to your health.

Minnesota is below average when it comes to humidity. *The Statistical Abstract of the United States* lists 41 cities with more summer-time humidity levels than Minneapolis-St. Paul, and just 25 cities with less—5 of them by a single percentage point. Normal Minneapolis-St. Paul afternoon humidity in July is 54 percent. That's bad? Or just about right?

So MUCH FOR MINNESOTA NICE.

Bunk	Debunk

"We've got dry heat down here. (And you don't.)" Or: "We've got cool heat. (And you don't.)"

You've also got Sun Sear. The sun gets a direct-angle shot at your hide come summer down there. Ol' Sol will fry you on the rippling pavement where you stand. That's *hot* heat, Pal, any way you cook it.

"It's not the temperature, it's the Windchill."

Windchill is not the horror it's made out to be. First off, winds are not constant, they gust. And you can get out of the wind (much like finding shade in summer). And Windchills are offset by radiant heat from the Sun (the Sun Sear Factor).

"Minnesotans are up to their butts in snow half the year."

Annual snowfall is 49.8 inches in the metropolitan Twin Cities where 54% of Minnesotans reside. Spread over a winter, your butt would have to be pretty low to the ground for snow to be up to it. That's hardly more snow than Pittsburgh, half as much as Buffalo (NY), and a quarter less than Cleveland. Great Falls, Spokane, Portland, and Burlington, (VT) all get more snow than drops in Twin City driveways. About 95% of all

Bunk	**Debunk**

Minneapolis-St. Paul snow falls within three months, between December 15 and March 15. Minnesota snowfalls enhance winter recreation, are a godsend to farmers, and an abhorrence to crabgrass.

"People hibernate all winter long in Minnesota."

There's more to do during Minnesota winters than in most other states, and Minnesotans do it: It's better than brown grass, or slush, as in some other places. Winter here provides a variety of recreational activities that Minnesotans take to—indoors *and* out.

"You're pale."

Chances are you're not the crinkled one in this conversation.

"It's cold, cold, cold."

The average year-round *minimum* temperature for Minneapolis-St. Paul is 35.3 degrees F. Some cities touting warmth over the Twin Cities like you wouldn't believe, are: Chicago and Omaha (both averaging 39.5), Detroit (39.0), Albany (36.6); Hartford (36.2), and Portland (35.8). My, what a difference. Some Metro's with

Bunk	Debunk

colder average minimum temperatures are: Reno (NV) (34.7), Sioux Falls (SD) (34.2), Cheyenne (WY) (33.2), Concord, (MA) (33.1), and Bismark, (ND) (29.4). Surprised?

"It's cold, cold, *colder*."

The mean high temperature in Minneapolis-St. Paul, January through February, is 24 degrees F. For December it's 27. March it's 37. Higher than you (and they) thought. Right? Wanna compare some "warmer" cities? Look it up. The area is not among the Coldest Cities listed by the National Center for Educational Statistics—nor Snowiest either.

"Snow, oh no."

Without snow winter would be a drag. You know, like it is in Brownoutville. You ski downhill on it, ski cross-country on it, toboggan and sled on it, snowmobile on it, snow-shoe hike and jog on it. Build snowmen with it, throw snowballs, build forts, make angels and have white Christmases with it. Plus, there's just the soul-cleansing beauty of it.

Bunk	Debunk
"It's hot, hot, hot."	**The Minneapolis-St. Paul average high temperature in July is 84 degrees.** Combined with normal mid-day humidity (54%), average July breezes, and Sun Sear of less intensity than southerly places, it's comfort, comfort, comfort.
"Minnesota mosquitoes will carry you away."	**During daylight hours you have to stir the bush to rouse the little beasties.** They're annoying at dusk all right, but diminish to mildly pesky after dark. And, there's DEET to give them flight.
"You can only golf three months a year."	**Double that, sandbagger.** Golfers routinely take to the links in the Minneapolis-St. Paul area from early April to late October. That's six-plus months at last count.
"Our place (city) is growing like mad." (Meaning: we're hot and you're not.)	**Our place is growing like *sane.*** The Twin Cities shows the strongest growth rate among northern tier major metropolitan centers. Now, wanna compare quality of life studies with Minnesota cities? You lose.
"There's nothing to do."	**Ya gotta be kidd'n.**

Star-studded Natives.

Here's a list of Minnesota high achievers to dazzle 'em with. Watch their eyes widen as you tick them off. Just don't admit that you were equally as surprised at this imposing menu of homers as they'll be.

Music mavens:

Andrews Sisters
Cab Calloway
Eddie Cochran
Lamont Cranston
Bob Dylan
Hüsker Dü
Jimmie "Jam" Harris
The Jets
Michael Johnson
Leo Kottke
Peggy Lee
Terry Lewis
The Magnolias
Anne Murray (Just seeing if you're paying attention.)
Eugene Ormandy
The Entertainer Formerly Known as Prince
The Replacements
Butch Thompson
Soul Asylum
The Suburbs
Bobby Vee
The Wolverines
Yanni
Peter Yarrow (of Peter, Paul and what's-her-name).
Mary McGregor (Her voice, Peter's tune, a
    big hit. Remember the song?)

Actors, entertainers, artists, communicators:
(Show-biz glitz drops 'em to their knees.)

Eddie Albert
Loni Anderson
Louie Anderson
Richard Dean Anderson
Richard Arlen
James Arness
Tom Arnold
John Astin
Lew Ayres
Marlon Brando (OK, he just attended
    Minnesota's Shattuck Military Academy—
    before getting kicked out.)
Richard Carlson (He lead three lives.)
The Coen brothers (Ethan and Joel)
Arlene Dahl
Joan Davis
Julia Duffy
William Demarest
Richard Dix
Mike Farrell
Ed Flanders
Henry Fonda (Well, he went to the University
    of Minnesota, anyway.)
Al Franken
Mark Frost
Judy Garland
Peter Graves
Scott Hansen
Tippi Hedren
George Roy Hill
Garrison Keillor
Dorothy Lyman

Linda Kelsey
Jessica Lange
Pinky Lee
E.G. Marshall
Randy Merriman
Margaret Morris
Chris Mulkey
Brent Mussberger (OK, he just attended
    Shattuck—and actually made it.)
Gena Lee Nolin (Worth watching on that bay.)
Gordon Parks
Harry Reasoner
Nate Richert
Marion Ross
Jane Russell
Winona Ryder
Eric Sevareid
Kevin Sorbo (Powerful!)
Ann Southern
Lea Thompson
Mike Todd
Robert Vaughn
Jesse "The Body" Ventura
Richard Widmark
William Windom
Gig Young

Sports stars.

Minnesota Heat has emphasized home-grown
athletes here, not Minnesota-team stalwarts who
came to play and stayed—the likes of Carl Eller,
Jim Marshall, Mick Tinglehoff, Chuck Foreman,
Bob Allison, Tony Oliva, Zoilo Versalles and a host
of others. There are six we just had to include,
though. Track the double stars and you'll see why.

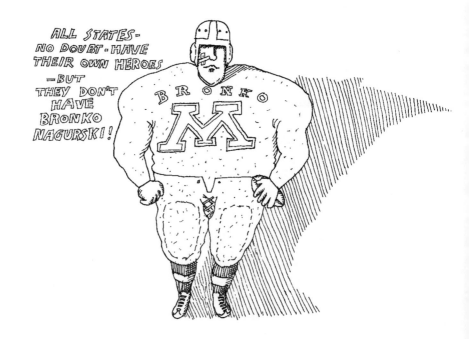

ALL STATES - NO DOUBT - HAVE THEIR OWN HEROES — BUT THEY DON'T HAVE BRONKO NAGURSKI!

Baseball:

Jim Eisenreich
Kent Hrbek
Dave Goltz
Jerry Koosman
Tim Laudner
Roger Maris
Paul Molitor
Jack Morris
Greg Olson
Kirby Puckett**
Terry Steinbach
Dave Winfield

Basketball:

Randy Breuer
Sam Jacobson
Tony Jaros
Janet Karvonen
John Kundla
Kevin McHale (Named one of the 50 top
players in NBA history.)
Chuck Mencel
Vern Mikkelsen
George Mikan** (He joins Kevin on the NBA
Top 50 list.)
Mark Olberding
Jim Peterson
Whitey Skoog

Football:

Bernie Bierman
Dave Casper
Keith Fahnhorst
Paul Giel

THERE'LL NEVER BE ANOTHER BRONKO NAGURSKI

THERE'LL NEVER BE ANOTHER BERNIE BIERMAN

THERE'LL NEVER BE ANOTHER PAUL GIEL

THERE'LL NEVER BE ANOTHER VIC KULBITSKI

THERE'LL NEVER BE ANOTHER CLAYTON TONNAMAKER
OR
GORDY SOLTAU
OR
PINKY McNAMARA
OR
BOB McNAMARA

THERE'LL NEVER BE ANOTHER SID HARTMAN

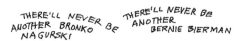

DURING THE HALF OF THE '47 MINNESOTA INDIANA GAME BRUCE "PUDGE" SCHMIDT TOOK THE FIELD AND, FROM MEMORY, RECITED EVERY FOOTBALL PLAYER, AND COACH, WHO EVER PLAYED AT MINNESOTA.
NOT TOO SHABBY, BRUCE.

Vern Gagne
Bud Grant
Paul Krause**
Karl Mecklenburg
Bronko Nagurski (NFL Hall of Fame *charter member,* no less.)
Alan Page**
Gordy Soltau
Bruce Smith (The Heisman Trophy one.)
Clayton Tonnemaker
Steve Walsh
Murray Warmath**
Bud Wilkinson

Hockey:

Frankie Brimsek ("Mr. Zero".)
Herb Brooks (Gophers coach, Olympic coach—
   Do you believe in miracles? *Yes!)*
Aaron Broten
Neal Broten
Billy Christian
Steve Christoff
Paul Holmgren
Reed Larson
John Mariucci
John Mayasich
Bill Nyrop
Mike Ramsey
Eric Strobel
Doug Woog
Ken Yackel

Tennis/Golf:

Jeanne Arth (Wimbledon champion.)
Patty Berg (LPGA great, one of its founders.)

James Harris (National Amateur golf champion.)
Tim Herron (PGA big hitter.)
Tom Lehman (Need you ask?)
David Wheaton (International tennis star.)

Other Sportsters:

Dick Beardsley (Marathon champion and
   record holder.)
Jim Bauer (National x-c ski champion.)
Fritz Carlson (Boston Marathon winner.)
Minnesota Fats (Notorious pool hustler.)
Vern Gagne (*World* wrestling champion.)
Jack Gibbons (Jack Dempsey challenger.)
John S. Johnson (World champ speed skater.)
Janice Klecker (World-class marathoner.)
Bob Kempainen (Olympic marathoner.)
Greg LeMond** (Three-time winner, Tour
   de France.)
Cindy Nelson (Olympic ski medalist.)
Tasha Nelson (U.S. ski champion.)
The Great Dan Patch (All-time carriage
   racing steed.)
Amy Peterson (Multi-medal Olympian speedskater.)
Jill Trenary (World champion figure skater.)
John Roethlisberger (Olympic gymnast.)
Gar Wood (Speedboat champion.)

**The adopted six in the mix:

George Mikan, named the outstanding player of
the first fifty years of basketball, stands tall in the
Twin Cities community. Greg LeMond (the only
American ever to win at Tour deFrance), not
spinning his wheels, is involved in motor racing
and other business ventures in these parts. Alan
Page, football Hall of Famer and NFL MVP, is a

Minnesota Supreme Court Justice. Paul Krause, former Vikings free safety and NFL all-time leader in pass-interceptions, is a successful land developer and an elected Dakota County commissioner. Murray Warmath came a long way to Minnesota, where he struggled, endured, and triumphed. Two Rose Bowls plus a should-have-been Big 10 championship denied by zebras with his best team of all. Thanks, Coach. Kirby Puckett, Minnesota's all-time most popular athlete, couldn't possibly reside anywhere else—they named a street after him.

Somethin' else, sports fans: St. Paul, is the only city in the nation boasting two native sons to get 3,000 hits in major league baseball—those redoubtable boys of summer, Winfield and Molitor. As if by providence, both did it wearing Minnesota Twins uniforms. Both were Golden Gopher stalwarts, as well. Winnie collected his 3,000th hit on September 16, 1993. Mollie got his three years to the day after his compatriot did, becoming only the 21st player in the majors to reach that milestone.

Bench sitters:

Pierce Butler, U.S. Supreme Court Justice, 1922-1939.

William O. Douglas, U.S. Supreme Court Justice, 1939-1975 (Longest term ever served on the high bench).

Warren Burger, U.S. Supreme Court, Chief Justice, 1969-1986.

Harry Blackmun, U.S. Supreme Court Justice, 1970—.

WE'RE KINDA
PROUD OF SINCLAIR LEWIS
IN MINNESOTA

OH YEAH, "LUCKY SINCLAIR" AND
THE SPIRIT OF ST. LOUIS.

Authors awesome:

(Skulkers may require recognition coaching, here.)

C. C. Beck (They may know his super hero, but do they know what SHAZAM is an acronym for? Do *you*?)

Louise Ercrich (Love cures.)

Frederick Feikema (Lord of the wilds.)

F. Scott Fitzgerald (They'll know he's important, what with the front initial and all.)

Thomas Gifford (Talk about Windchill Factors.)

Judith Guest (She's *ordinary people*.)

John Hassler (Down home guy.)

Colleen Hitchcock (Lyrical ascent.)

Siri Hustvedt (Hot stuff, kinda scary.)

Garrison Keillor (*Minnesota Heat* hasn't said it all about Minnesota.)

Sinclair Lewis (*Main street* kinda guy.)

Harvey Mackay (Swims with the sharks.)

Howard Mohr (Talks the talk.)

Sigurd Olson (Tunes of the wild.)

Robert Persig (Zen and maintenance metaphors.)

Ole Rolvaag (Giants of yore and lore.)

Carl Rowan (Words of syndication.)

John Sandford (*Prey* tell.)

Harrison Salisbury (Pulitzer man.)

Charles Schulz (Works for Peanuts.)

Max Shulman (Humor too sophisticated for 'em?)

Wallace Stegner (Rocks atop a candy mound.)

Robert Penn Warren (Poetry over their heads?)

Laura Ingalls Wilder (Little house, big prairie.)

Honorables of mention:

(If you thought you had to coach them on authors, wait'l the Nobel Laureates come up.)

Eugenie Anderson (Ms. First-Ms. Ambassador.)
Paul Bunyan (Mr. Big.)
Norman Borlaug (Mr. Nobel Agronomist.)
Curt Carlson (Mr. Radisson-and-more.)
Betty Crocker (Ms. American Pantry.)
Pillsbury Doughboy (Mr. American Pantry.)
J. Paul Getty (Mr. Bucks.)
Jolly Green Giant (Mr. Big II.)
Don Herbert (Mr. Wizard.)
Hubert Humphrey (Mr. Mayor, Mr. Senator,
    Mr. Vice President, Mr. President-almost,
    Mr. Professor, Mr. Senator-once-again,
    Mr. Nice Guy.)
James J. Hill (Mr. Railroad.)
Frank Kellogg (Mr. Nobel-of-peace.)
Edward Kendall (Mr. Nobel-of-discovery.)
Sister Elizabeth Kenny (Ms. Nurse of Nurses.)
Charles Lindbergh (Mr. Lone Eagle.)
Charles and William Mayo (Messrs. Clinic.)
Eugene McCarthy (Mr. Voice-to-a-generation.)
Walter Mondale (Mr. Attorney General,
    Mr. Senator, Mr. Vice President,
    Mr. Presidential Candidate, Mr. Ambassador,
    Mr. Things-yet-to-come.)
Gen. Lauris Norstad (Mr. NATO.)
Robert M. Page (Mr. Radar.)
Richard Sears (Mr. Retailer.)
Harold Stassen (Mr. Governor, Mr. Presidential
    Candidate, Mr. Presidential Candidate,
    Mr. Presidential Candidate...)

C. E. Wickman (Mr. Greyhound.)
Roy Wilkins (Mr. NAACP.)

Have we fudged? Our accent is on natives of Minnesota, and in most cases that's so. But we've also included some transplanted residents who made their mark in Gopher-land in a big way. (How do you *not* include Hubert Humphrey? Or Bud Grant?) Our apologies to those we've omitted. Maybe next time around.

Minnesota Firsts and Foremosts.

If you've been paying attention (you have haven't you?) you're already familiar with much of the material under this heading. But here it is in easy-to-find, condensed form for rapid reply. Besides, you should be more comfortable coming to grips with Minnesota "firsts" at this stage of the game if *Minnesota Heat* has done anything for you at all. So we've slipped a few more in. Ready? Go get 'em.

Softball. Around the turn of the 20th Century, kittenball bounced out of Minneapolis and later evolved into softball.

Water skiing. Minnesotan Ralph Samuelson did it first—on Lake Peppin, near Red Wing, MN.

In-line skates. They rolled out from St. Louis Park, MN.

Snowmobiles. Polaris Industries, Roseau, MN, turned the "iron dogs" loose in 1954.

Ski boots. Minnesota's Rosemount, Inc. was first to develop plastic ski boots. Its "Elephant Foot" was the first rear-entry ski boot, too.

Radio jingles. The first singing commercial aired in Minneapolis, in 1924.

City lights. Minnesota Brush Electric was the first company in the U.S. to generate electric arc lighting from a central station, in Minneapolis.

First Volunteers. The Minnesota First was the first volunteer regiment to enlist with the Union in the Civil War. It was number one in battle, too.

Airline travel. Northwest Airlines introduced the first closed-cabin commercial flight, in 1926.

Atlantic air crossing. Charles Lindbergh was first to fly across the pond to Paris, in 1927. A ways from Little Falls, MN.

Shopping malls. Southdale, Edina, MN, became the first enclosed mall in the land, in 1956. Mall of America became the biggest, in 1992.

Skyways. The first two skyways in the nation bridged downtown streets in Minneapolis. One-hundred skyways now link 94 city blocks in the Twin Cities. More coming.

Home thermostats. Minneapolis Honeywell dialed them into our homes.

Puffed cereal. It popped up in Minnesota, in 1901.

Scotch Tape. Minnesota Mining & Manufacturing invented it.

Magnetic recording tape. 3M was first to develop it for market.

Post-it Notes. 3M invented these puppies, too.

Minnesota medicine. Medical breakthoughs include open heart surgery, liver transplants, pancreas transplants, pacemakers, CT scans, respirating machines, and certified nursing schools. HMO's were conceived and grew healthy in Minnesota.

Treatment centers. Hazeltine, the first alcohol abuse center, became the "Minnesota Model" for treatment centers across the nation.

Smoking bans. They cleared the air first in Minnesota. They first *took* to the air from here, too—flying Northwest Airlines.

Corporate tithings. Firms throughout Minnesota donate 5% of their pretax earning to educational institutions, arts, and social services.

Education. Minnesota ranks first in percentage of students graduated from high school, those going on to college, and literacy of population.

Voter turnout. Minnesota is commonly first in voter turnout for president.

Recycling. Minnesota recycles 44% of its solid waste materials—highest percentage among states.

Tough sledd'n. Minnesotan Will Steger was the first to cross Antarctica by dog sled.

Tough sail'n. In 1979, Minnesota adventurer Gerry Spiess became the only person to cross the Atlantic in a keel-less (10-foot) sailboat.

Nordic track'n. From Chaska, MN, came the x-c skier that got home exercise on a new track.

The ice cream sandwich. It came from Blue Earth, MN. (No, it didn't occur naturally one wintry day.)

I SCREAM SANDWICH..
YOU SCREAM SANDWICH...

Quality of Life. In Gallup interviews, Minneapolis was selected as offering the best quality of life in the midwest. Minnesota, or one or more of its cities, consistently ranks in the top group of quality of life studies. (Does Skulkerville?)

Generation-X life. *Swing* magazine named Minneapolis one of the "The 10 Best Places to Live" for young folk.

Education. Minnesota consistently scores among the top three states on college entrance exams.

Performing arts. The Twin Cities metropolitan area is second to New York City in number of cultural events and performing arts groups.

Movie Making. *Hollywood Reporter* lists Minnesota as one of the five hottest locales for movies.

MTM House. So, where did Mary Tyler Moore "live" all those glorious TV years? In a charming Victorian home on Kenwood Parkway in south Minneapolis. You should see it.

Wildlife. Minnesota's wolf population is the largest in the lower 48 states. Same for bald eagles. Same for moose. (No, it's not *mooses*).

Fortune 500 companies. Fourteen Minnesota companies are on the Fortune 500 list of top U.S. publicly held companies of 1996. And, Minnesota is home to Cargill, the largest privately owned company in the country.

Jobs and culture. *Fortune* scores Minneapolis fourth on its 1996 "15 best-U.S.-Cities".

Publishing. Minnesota is third in book publishing, behind New York and California.

Financial enterprise. There are more millionaires per capita in metro Minneapolis than in any other major metropolitan area in the U.S. Minnesota has more millionaires per capita than Texas. Same goes for those other "virtuoso" states.

Shoreline. Minnesota has more shoreline than California, Texas and Florida combined—over 90,000 miles of it.

Lakes. Minnesota has more lakes than any other state: 15,291. More than 95% of Minnesotans live within five miles of recreational waters.

Golf. There are more golf courses per capita in Minnesota than any other state except North Dakota. More than 20% of Minnesotans golf—second highest among all states.

Fishing. Anglers catch 25 million fish annually in Minnesota—more than 20 fish for every million-plus licenses issued.

Boating. Minnesota has the most boat owners per capita (one in six own one or more boats). It's number one in outboard motors, outright.

Hunting. Minnesota is first in total hunting licenses issued annually.

While you're hot, why not pile on with a burst of Attrition Trivia before they have a chance to recover? Flip to page 110 and keep on squeezing 'em off.

DUCK HUNTING'S A VERY POPULAR SPORT IN MINNESOTA

Keep Skulkers at bay at home and away, with *Minnesota Heat* Take-alongs.

innesota Heat Take-alongs available here are specially designed to bolster and support you in dealing with skulkers—on their turf or yours.

No tantalizing photographs (you know what caps look like). No tear-out forms, no self-addressed ordering envelopes. Matter of fact, you're pretty much on your own when you order *Minnesota Heat* merchandise. Use your own envelope, along with a note as to what items you'd like, and your personal check or money order at the ridiculously low, direct-mail, discount prices listed. Would *Minnesota Heat* send you shoddy merchandise after putting you through all that? It wouldn't be Minnesotan, now would it?

Minnesota Heat luggage tags.

Don't leave home without them. Skulkers picking you up at the airport will see you're a Minnesotan not to be trifled with—warns you're prepared for their verbal jabs. These plastic tags display *Minnesota Heat* logo in three lustrous colors. Insert your business card in the pocket on the other side of tag, or use the standard I.D. card included, and you're on your way.

$7.95, set of four, plus shipping & handling. $6.95 for each additional set of four, plus shipping & handling.

Minnesota Heat baseball cap.

Don't turn this cap around backwards when you travel south—let visor shield your face from the blistering sun. Remember, *Heat Sear.* The embroidered 3-color *Minnesota Heat* logo will shield the rest of you from the you-know-who's. Six panel construction, 100% cotton crown with no buckram backing, washed natural color, matching cloth sizing band. Blue bill, grommets and button.

$14.95 plus shipping & handling.

Minnesota Heat embroidered T-shirt.

If this won't hold 'em off, nothing will. Shouts your defiance in un-Minnesota-like fashion—they won't be sure you really are one. *Minnesota Heat* logo is emblazoned over your heart in three colors. Sturdy weight 100% cotton, natural color. Specify Large or Extra Large.

$14.95 plus shipping & handling.

Minnesota Heat embroidered golf towel.

Lower your home-state handicap with *Minnesota Heat* golf towel prominently displayed on your bag. 3-color logo keeps skulkers off balance while you stay concentrated on your game. 16x26" tri-fold towel neatly attaches to your bag with centered grommet and clip. 100% cotton, 2-ply yarn-hemmed velour terry.

$14.95 plus shipping & handling.

Minnesota Heat **head band.**

Does wonders for your tennis game and other court-sport matches with opposing (and now distracted) skulkers. Use it running, too. Skulkers are everywhere, you know. Terry cotton elastic with embroidered *Minnesota Heat* logo in three colors.

$8.95 plus shipping & handling.

Geo-climatic Skulker **certification cards.**

Pass them out to Geo-climatic Skulkers you iden-tify. Puts them on notice that you've blown their cover (as if they ever had one). Standard business-card size. 3-color *Minnesota Heat* logo.

$6.95, pack of 15 cards, plus shipping & handling.
**$5.95 each additional pack of l5 cards,
plus shipping & handling.**

'Tis the MN Season, wall hanging.

You undoubtedly admired, and were thoroughly enthralled with, the lyric prose and tasteful look of *'Tis the MN Season* (page 108). Well, you can have your very own print—color embellished on pretty good picture stock, suitable for framing. At 5 x 7", *'Tis the MN Season* is easy to pack and take along to snowbird locales you visit. Adorn your wall at home with one, too. You never know when skulkers will drop in come summer.

$7.95 plus shipping & handling.
$6.95 each additional print, plus shipping & handling.

Be prepared, next time out. Send for your very own personal *Minnesota Heat* Take-alongs, today.

Mail-order prices in this book are valid through 1998. Most orders will be shipped within 5 working days of receipt, although unforeseen circumstances may delay things a bit. Hey, you expected Eddie Bauer service?

Eventually, we'd like to have *Minnesota Heat* merchandise in gift shops throughout Minnesota (and some other states, too)—even bookstores, if they'll let us in. You can wait for that to maybe happen, if you want. Whatever.

Minnesota Heat Take-alongs
Worksheet & Order Form

Make copies of this handy form before filling it out and you'll have an endless supply to send in for *Minnesota Heat* merchandise.

Customer Name _____

Street Address _____

City, State, Zip _____

Work Phone (____)_____ Home Phone (____) _____

	No. of Items	Price Each Item	MN Sales Tax	Total Price of Item(s)
Imprinted Luggage Tags				
Embroidered Baseball Cap			▓	
Embroidered T-shirt: ☐ Large ☐ XL			▓	
Embroidered Golf Towel				
Embroidered Head Band			▓	
Geo-climatic Skulker Cards				
'Tis the MN Season Wall Hanging				
Total Price All Items				

If ordering from Minnesota add 6.5% Minnesota State Sales Tax to cost of luggage tags, golf towels, Skulker cards and *'Tis the MN Season* prints.

If ordering from outside Minnesota, add appropriate state sales tax, if any.

Shipping & Handling (Do not include sales tax when calculating.)
Total purchase *less than* $14.95: add $1.75 to order.
Total purchase *of* $14.95: add $2.50 to order.
Total purchase *more than* $14.95: add $3.50 to order.

TOTAL	

Send check or money order to: **Minnesota Heat** Take-alongs
9135 Forest Hills Circle
Bloomington, MN 55437-1826

Final comments ...

You've noticed: *Minnesota Heat* raises some questions it doesn't completely answer, if at all. That would take more pages, and this book is expensive enough. Besides, this way you're left with something to ponder on a cold winter's night in front of a cozy fire.

You might find *Minnesota Heat* has erred on rare occasion—not on premise, of course, but technically. If you discover a lapse of this sort let us know at the *Take-alongs* address given. We'll try to set things right in the next printing. (See how optimistic we are.) Unlike Geo-climatic Skulkers you've encountered, *Minnesota Heat* aims for accuracy at all times.

...and a Charge!

How has *Minnesota Heat* done? Are you better prepared for those harassing Geo-climatic Skulkers than you were before—more aware, more knowledgeable, feeling better about life on the northern tier? Even so, it may take a few excursions away from home before you're able to stand off skulkers as effectively as you'd like. Don't be discouraged. It's new to you, long-practiced by them; and what comes naturally to them, doesn't to you. As we said in the beginning: it won't be easy, and not always pretty. But should you persevere, you will, however slowly, make strides. Like Henry Schoolcraft, you'll step across that great barrier span, once you've found your own "true source".
Wind and weather permitting.

THE LAST WORD